BORDERLINE PERSONALITY DISORDER

THE ULTIMATE GUIDE ON COGNITIVE BEHAVIORAL THERAPY. IMPROVE YOUR SOCIAL SKILLS WITH OVERCOMING DEPRESSION. STOP ANXIETY, REWIRE YOUR BRAIN, IMPROVE YOUR RELATIONSHIPS

BY JON POWER

Table of Contents

Introduction

"Borderline Personality Disorder (BPD) is a mode error and how one person interacts with others. This is the most commonly recognized personality disorder."

Generally, a person's personality disorder will be significantly different from the average person in terms of how he thinks, understands, feels or relates to others. Borderline Personality Disorder (BPD) is a condition in which emotions are difficult to manage. This means that people who experience BPD experience emotions emotionally and for a long time, and it is difficult for them to return to a stable baseline after an emotionally stimulating event.

This problem can lead to unconsciousness, poor self-image, stormy relationships and severe emotional reactions to stressors.

Borderline Personality Disorder is a mental health disorder that affects how you think and feel about yourself and others, leading to difficulties in everyday life. It includes self-image problems, difficulty handling emotions and behaviors, and a pattern of unstable relationships.

With the Borderline Personality Disorder, you have a severe fear of isolation or instability, and you may have problems with being alone. Still, inappropriate anger, fast and frequent mood swings can remove others, even though you want to have a loving and lasting relationship.

Borderline personality disorder usually begins in early adolescence. The condition is known to be worse in adolescence and may gradually improve with age. If you have a borderline personality disorder, don't despair. Many people with this disorder get better with treatment over time and can learn to live a satisfying life. Borderline Personality Disorder is a disease that involves different moods, self-image, and ongoing patterns of behavior.

These symptoms often result from good actions and problems in the relationship. Borderline Personality Disorder sufferers can experience severe episodes of anger, depression, and anxiety that can last for hours to days.

People with BPD are very sensitive. Some describe it as having an exposed nerve end. Small things can cause severe reactions. And once you are upset, you will have trouble calming down.

It is easy to understand how these emotional fluctuations and self-inconvenience create chaos and disappointment even in careless behavior in relationships.

You can say hurtful things or act in dangerous or inappropriate ways after which you will be guilty or ashamed. It's a traumatic cycle with no escape. But it is not so. There are effective BPD treatment and coping skills that can help you to feel better and better at controlling your thoughts, feelings and actions.

Usually, it has following symptoms:

Inappropriate or extremely emotional reactions

Highly emotional behavior

Unstable relationship history

Acute mood changes, sharp behavior, and extreme reactions can make it difficult for people to complete school education with borderline personality disorder, maintain permanent jobs, and maintain long, healthy relationships.

In addition to…

Moreover, Borderline Personality Disorder (BPD) is a mental illness that makes it difficult for a person to feel comfortable.

Causes difficulty controlling emotions and movements. It causes other people problems. Additionally, people with BPD have a high level of anxiety and anger and can easily take offense to other actions or sayings. People with BPD can struggle with hurtful thoughts and beliefs about themselves and other people.

This can cause discomfort in their work life, family life and social life. Some people with BPD harm themselves People have different opinions about BPD / EUPD, and this can be a controversial diagnosis. But, however you understand your experiences, and whatever terms you like to use (if any), the important thing to remember is the emotions and behaviors associated with BPD /

EUPD. It is very difficult to live with, and deserves understanding and support.

Chapter 1. What Is Borderline Personality Disorder?

I have committed this part to give you an unmistakable, effectively reasonable picture of BPD. On the slight off chance that you believe that you or somebody near you may have BPD, it is useful to know precisely what this implies.

Before you begin perusing this part, it is significant for you to realize that you can't determine yourself to have BPD. In spite of the fact that you may find out about a portion of the side effects of BPD and believe "That is me!" you should see an expert (an analyst, a specialist, or another person who analyze mental disarranges) make sense of whether you really have BPD.

Attempting to determine yourself to have a mental disorder is a lot of like attempting to determine yourself to have malignant growth or coronary illness. You need an expert to do it since you doubtlessly don't have the devices, abilities, or target perspective important to make the conclusion.

Also, in the event that you made an inappropriate finding, you probably won't get the correct sort of help. I have met with a few people who thought they had BPD yet ended up having some other disorder, similar to sorrow, bipolar confusion, or posttraumatic stress disorder.

Similarly, as the prescribed medicines for malignant growth are not quite the same as those for coronary illness, each mental or enthusiastic disorder requires an alternate treatment. Consequently, you'll have to ensure your conclusion is precise, and the best way to do this is to see an expert. Along these lines, utilize this section to realize what BPD is about and to show signs of improvement comprehension of the side effects of this disorder.

MENTAL DISORDERS, PERSONALITY DISORDERS, AND BPD

A personality disorder is essentially a dependable example of identifying with the world that doesn't work well indeed. Also, these disorders cause incredible pain and may make challenges seeing someone or lead to disorders arriving at objectives throughout everyday life, (for example, objectives including getting or keeping an ideal activity). There is a wide range of kinds of personality disorder, including avoidant, fanatical impulsive, needy, jumpy, schizoid, schizotypal, narcissistic, dramatic, standoffish, and, obviously, borderline personality disorder. Having a personality disorder ordinarily implies having a lot of disorders that have been with you for quite a while.

For the most part, you must be a grown-up to be determined to have a personality disorder. In any case, individuals determined to have a personality disorder as grown-ups will regularly say that they have battled with these disorders for whatever length of time that they can recall. Accordingly, we accept that numerous individuals have had these disorders since they were youngsters.

Having a personality disorder doesn't imply that you have an imperfect personality, have poor personality, or are a mean or unlikable individual. Essentially, the supposition that will be that individuals with personality disorder have something as a part of their characteristics that makes disorders for them and for others. Presently, we don't completely concur with this, for a couple of reasons.

Second, this term recommends that the disorder is within you and that on the slight off chance that you could just fix yourself everything would be typical. We can't help contradicting this perspective too. There is a great deal of proof that the earth, (for example, stress, injury, misuse, and other such factors) assumes a solid job in numerous mental disorders, including personality disorder. Furthermore, putting the disorder within you can make shame and critical responses with respect to others.

At long last, the term personality disorder likewise recommends that, in the event that you have a personality disorder, you have consistently had it (its piece of your personality, some portion of what makes you the individual you are) and you generally will have it. As you'll find in part 4, in any case, there is proof that BPD doesn't in every case keep going insofar as individuals might suspect it does. Along these lines, having BPD doesn't imply that you have an imperfect personality, or that you will consistently battle with the disorders you are having at this moment.

It just implies that you have an example of reasoning, feeling, and carrying on that might be blocking your capacity to have a high caliber

13

of life, prop your connections up securely, or arrive at your objectives. Entangling matters is the way that the DSM-IV-TR depends halfway on the possibility that mental disorder is a lot of like clinical sicknesses or maladies. The DSM-IV-TR utilizes an "infection model" for mental clutters, relating them to a pathology (brokenness) inside the individual (or in nature), much like you would with pneumonia, diabetes, or other such ailments. The disorder with this thought is that mental disorder doesn't appear to work similarly as illnesses do. In the first place, you can't "get" a mental disorder like you can get pneumonia. Second, dissimilar to illnesses, for example, diabetes, mental clutters have not been connected to any physical breakdown that may cause them. Third, a considerable lot of the side effects of the explicit disorder, (for example, wretchedness) are likewise found in numerous different disorders, so the line between these disarranges is foggy. Interestingly, it is obvious to doctors when an individual has diabetes versus bosom malignant growth. Fourth, analyze depend on what you do, think, or feel.

The supposition that will be that sure things that you may do, think or feel would demonstrate the nearness of a hidden disorder. That is an entire large jump to make. Researchers can't glimpse inside somebody's body or cerebrum and locate a basic disorder, as they do when they find a carcinogenic tumor. Fifth, the sickness model, similar to the term personality disorder, puts the disorder for the most part within you. As we depict beneath, in the event that you have BPD, a significant number of the disorders that you battle with are identified with disorders in the earth, as opposed to disorders that exist within

14

you. Besides, the progressions that you may need to make so as to be more joyful may really include changing nature or changing how you act, think, or feel. Consequently, we accept that what you do, think, and feel are considerably more significant than whether you have confusion.

HISTORY OF BPD

The broadly held view was that there were two huge classifications of mental disorders or disorders. One classification, called despondency, included patients who knew about the real world however who had passionate disorders, for example, sadness or nervousness disorder.

The other classification, psychosis, included patients who had abnormal musings and encounters, (for example, visualizations) that were not situated as a general rule, and these patients were determined to have cluttered, for example, schizophrenia. Patients who didn't have disorders sufficiently genuine to be marked crazy (as such, their reasoning and encounters were to a great extent situated in all actuality), however, were too disturbed to even consider being called masochists were placed into the borderline classification.

Therapists utilized the term fringe for patients who made some hard memories seeing both the great and terrible characteristics in individuals simultaneously, who drove insecure and clamorous lives, and who were regularly genuinely troubled. A considerable lot of these perspectives about BPD came straightforwardly from perceptions of a set number of patients and did not depend on logical research. Since those early days, specialists have led various examinations. Discoveries from these examinations have distinguished numerous significant characteristics that makeup what we presently call borderline personality disorder, including challenges overseeing feelings, indiscreet conduct, and relationship and personality disorders.

Individuals with BPD are never again thought to verge on psychosis and anxiety. Science is helping us keep the thoughts regarding BPD that appear to be valid and dispose of the old thoughts regarding BPD that doesn't appear to be exact.

THE SYMPTOMS AND FEATURES OF BORDERLINE PERSONALITY DISORDER

BPD is a turmoil of insecurity and disorders with feelings. Individuals with BPD are insecure in their feelings, their reasoning, their connections, their personality, and their conduct. Individuals with BPD have rough connections and are regularly scared of being surrendered. Inwardly, individuals with BPD feel like they are on an exciting ride, with their feelings going here and there suddenly.

They may likewise experience difficulty with outrage (either having outrage upheavals or being so terrified of outrage that they maintain a strategic distance from it totally). Individuals with BPD act imprudently (they act rapidly without intuition) when they are disturbed, and they now and then endeavor suicide and take part in self-hurt. Frequently, individuals with BPD experience difficulty making sense of what their identity is, and they here and there experience difficulty thinking plainly and staying grounded when they are worried.

A compelling treatment for BPD goes does:

FEELING DYSREGULATION

This alludes to insecure feelings (counting quick state of mind changes) and trouble overseeing feelings. Individuals with BPD battle with their feelings and are regularly overpowered by them. Truth be told, a few specialists have said that feeling dysregulation is the most significant disorder for individuals with BPD. In reality, a few people accept that the majority of the disorders that individuals with BPD battle with are brought about by feeling dysregulation. Temperamental feelings and mind-sets and trouble controlling resentment are the two manifestations of BPD that fall under this classification.

TEMPERAMENTAL EMOTIONS AND MOODS

Individuals with BPD regularly respond to things that probably won't influence others so firmly. For example, on the slight off chance that you have BPD, you may be handily furious about things that an individual's state or do, or you may find that you get worried more effectively than others. Only a little basic or opposing look may be sufficient to toss you into an enthusiastic spiral. Since individuals with BPD respond genuinely to such a large number of things, they regularly find that their feelings go all over like an exciting ride. They may feel glad one moment, and afterward miserable or irate the following moment. Extreme Anger or Difficulty Controlling Anger

INTENSE ANGER OR DIFFICULTY CONTROLLING ANGER IS ANOTHER FEATURE OF BPD.

Individuals with BPD might be effectively aggravated or infuriated by things that probably won't agitate others.

They may likewise be not able to control themselves when they blow up—tossing things, hollering at individuals, or feeling so devoured by rage that they don't have a clue what to do. In spite of the fact that outrage is one measure for BPD, we have seen, in working with individuals who have BPD that the feelings of disgrace, pity, and blame are regularly a lot more grounded and harder to adapt to. A few people with BPD appear to invest more energy being furious with themselves than with any other person.

RELATIONAL DYSREGULATION

Relational dysregulation implies experiencing difficulty with associations with others. It doesn't imply that you are an awful or unlikable individual. Indeed, individuals with BPD are regularly very enchanting, drawing in, fascinating, and delicate. By the by, they will in general battle in their connections in two essential ways: temperamental connections and dread of relinquishment.

PRECARIOUS AND INTENSE RELATIONSHIPS

Individuals with BPD regularly have "rough" connections that are riotous and crazy. In fact, their passionate force here and there makes it difficult for them to manage connections. On the slight off chance that you have BPD, you may find that occasionally things go fantastically well in your connections, and on different occasions, everything appears to self-destruct. You might be cheerful, in adoration, and thrilled one minute, and the following minute you may feel outraged and disdain and have miserable contemplations about your connections.

The essential thought is that connections, similar to feelings, appear to be an exciting ride, and they move rapidly to and fro between being great and downright awful. In the event that you have BPD, your connections may likewise include numerous contentions, battles, and even physical or psychological mistreatment.

CONDUCT DYSREGULATION

Conduct dysregulation implies that your conduct is wild (and possibly hurtful or unsafe) and is negatively affecting your life. Individuals with BPD regularly battle with this disorder in two essential manners: unsafe hasty conduct and self-hurt.

SELF AND IDENTITY DYSREGULATION

With self and personality dysregulation, an individual doesn't have a reasonable or stable feeling of who the individual in question is and can likewise feel void a significant part of the time.

SUBJECTIVE DYSREGULATION

With subjective dysregulation, an individual encounters negative reasoning and additionally a separation from self or reality when the individual is worried. It is critical to note here that these sorts of disorders are not generally there and happen predominantly when individuals with BPD are under a great deal of pressure or are truly disturbed.

SUSPICIOUS THOUGHTS OR DISSOCIATION WHEN EXPERIENCING STRESS

One disorder right now suspicious, negative, or "distrustful" pondering others' intentions. On the slight off chance that you battle with this disorder, it doesn't imply that you are silly, schizophrenic, or insane. It implies that when you are worried you begin to turn out to be particularly suspicious or stressed over how others feel about you. You may begin to accept that individuals are attempting to be mean to you, exploit you, or mischief you here and there.

You may likewise believe that individuals are taking a gander at you and thinking negative or critical contemplations about you, (for example, "He's fat," "She's revolting," "I don't care for her"). These encounters will, in general, happen when you are under pressure or are feeling vexed, yet they don't occur frequently when things are going easily. The other part of psychological dysregulation is separation. Separation is the experience of being looked at, scattered, in a foggy mental state, not mindful of your environment, or feeling as though you are not inside your body.

A few people portray feeling as though they are drifting to the roof and looking down on their bodies and the individuals around them. At the point when present in BPD, separation happens under pressure. Separation can really be an approach to get away from trouble. On the slight off chance that your manager fires you, and you feel apprehensive, restless, and irate, you may look at intellectually for a brief period so as to escape from your disorders or your misery.

The disorder with separating, obviously, is that it doesn't unravel anything, and you may do things when you are separating that are hazardous, (for example, suicide endeavors) or that you don't recollect a while later (for instance, dangerous single night rendezvous).

HOW DO YOU FIND OUT WHETHER YOU HAVE BPD?

As we talked about over, the most ideal approach to decide if you have BPD is to meet with an expert who is able to make analyze. A few distinct sorts of psychological well-being experts make analyze, including specialists and clinicians. Therapists are clinical specialists with specific preparation in prescription based and mental medicines.

The two therapists and analysts are regularly in a decent situation to lead an intensive evaluation and make a conclusion. Others who cause findings to incorporate social laborers, individuals with graduate degrees in brain science, or individuals with graduate degrees in guiding brain science.

We prescribe that you look for an expert with preparing and involvement in personality disorder and that you get a careful evaluation. Since BPD includes a long-standing example of identifying with the world (and is something that numerous individuals have battled with for the duration of their lives), the way toward diagnosing BPD may take some time.

In spite of the fact that it tends to be difficult to be tolerant when you truly need to discover what's up with you, a substantial determination is significant, and it might require a few arrangements and a great deal of talking. It is likewise significant that the expert you work with sees how to recognize BPD from different scatters that may look like BPD, for example, bipolar turmoil or significant sadness

Chapter 2. Symptoms Of Borderline Personality Disorder

People with BPD experience widespread mood swings and may experience instability and insecurity. Borderline Personality Disorder affects how you feel about yourself, how you relate to others, and how you are treated. Not everyone experiences borderline personality disorder.

Borderline Personality Disorder (BPD) sufferers can experience mood swings and have uncertainty about how they view themselves and their role in the world.

Borderline personality disorder sufferers also want to see things over and over, like all good or bad. Other people's opinions about them can change rapidly. An individual who is viewed as a friend one day may be considered an enemy the other day or a traitor.

These changing emotions can lead to intense and unstable relationships. Some people experience only a few symptoms, while others have many symptoms. Symptoms can be triggered by seemingly common occurrences. For example, victims of borderline personality disorder may be angry and upset at the slightest separation from people they feel close to, such as traveling on business trips.

Depending on the severity and frequency of symptoms and their age and their illness, how long they last. According to the Diagnostic and Statistical Manual Diagnostic Framework, some of the major signs and symptoms may include:

Great efforts by friends and family to avoid giving up real or imaginary.

Unstable personal relationships that alternate between ideologies such as;

"I'm in love!"

"I hate it"

Chronic feelings of anger or emptiness.

Inappropriate, severe or uncontrollable anger .This - often followed by shame and guilt.

Irrational Feelings your Disconnected from your own thoughts or feelings of identity, or "out of body" feelings of anxiety and stress related to stress. Severe episodes of stress can also lead to short psychological episodes.

Taking extreme steps to avoid severe fear of departure, even real or imagined separation or rejection.

Rapid changes in self-identity and self-image that involve changing goals and values, and making yourself feel bad or as if you no longer exist.

Stress-related paranoia and periods of contact with reality, from a few minutes to a few hours

Safeguarding success by influencing and treating risky behaviors, such as gambling, reckless driving, unsafe sex, spousal, binge eating or drug use, or leaving a good job or ending a positive relationship.

In response to the dangers of suicide or the fear of being treated or hurt, often separated or rejected.

Extensive mode lasts from a few hours to a few days, which can include intense joy, irritability, embarrassment or anxiety.

The ongoing feelings of emptiness

Inappropriate, severe anger, such as repeated loss of temper, sarcasm or bitterness, or physical confrontation.

Attempts to avoid giving up real or imagined, such as starting an intimate (physical or emotional) relationship or hoping to break off contact with someone

Impressive and often dangerous behaviors, such as spending troubles, having unprotected sex, substance abuse, reckless driving, and eating foods. If this behavior occurs primarily during a high mood or energy period, this mode may be a symptom of a defect - not a disturbance of the status quo.

Frequent thoughts of suicidal behavior or threats

Severe and highly variable mode with each event lasting from a few hours to a few days

Chronic feelings of emptiness

Inappropriate, intense anger or difficulty controlling anger

Hard to trust, which is sometimes with irrational fear of other people's intentions

Feelings of customization, such as the feeling of being cut off from yourself, seeing yourself from outside one's body, or the feeling of being unrealistic

Explained Symptoms

Because of the fear that other people will abandon them. Because of this, they can leave people who can't leave other people - in situations when other people will not feel it or take it personally.

The Borderline Personality Disorder is characterized by emotional disorder, which means an immediate, repetitive, and traumatic mood that is beyond the control of the victim. This problem makes it difficult for individuals with a problem to form and maintain relationships. They also face difficulties in controlling their own disorderly and careless behavior and often come up with ideas about who they are.

People who suffer from borderline personality disorder often have a history of intense relationships that start and end very suddenly. Often, this is due to two things:

Their fear of being abandoned

Their tendency to scold quickly and then to criticize other people

However, for the first time when another student refused to offer to be social, the young woman was terrified and hurt. He suddenly suspected that his new friend was leaving him and beat up another student, beat him and accused his friend of leaving him. Understandably, the other student ended the relationship.

For those struggling with borderline personality disorder, such episodes occur frequently and can be overwhelming. Severe emotions such as fear, distress, anxiety, anger, sadness and embarrassment can persist for a few hours as long as they can last for a few days.

However, when people are angry and overwhelmed, victims of borderline personality disorder also hesitate. Some people engage in tasks such as cutting their arms and legs and other forms of suicide. People may engage in the following:

Drugs & Alcohol excessively

Shopping they can't afford

Gamble excessively

Having unhealthy eating habits

Benching & Cleaning

In more frustrating situations, the person may try to commit suicide or think about suicide in detail. Most people involved in this problem are constantly testing their own relationships for problems and expect to be deserted by other people. They want to categorize themselves, others, and things into any "all good" or "all bad" classes with no middle ground.

This is why small problems can often lead to the end of a relationship. Yet, despite how quickly their relationship ends, many people suffering from borderline personality disorder are actually afraid of being lonely because they think they are unable to cope with the problems themselves. Borderline personality disorder in combat can be very tiring and disturbing.

People with this problem suffer from severe physical, emotional and psychological pain at all times. They are not even sure who they are. In one minute the person can think of himself as a good person, and in the next minute he will think of himself as bad and poor. Thoughts about other people also fluctuate rapidly. That person wants to trust others, but at the same time, he doesn't think other people are trustworthy. All this confusion can easily make a person feels:

Empty

Sad

Hollow

With the aggravation of disturbances, people struggling with borderline personality disorder sometimes feel like they leave their bodies in times of stress and can't remember what happened. These serious periods of loneliness only increase the unstable feeling of their self. Likewise, and equally disturbing, there is a period of deception that can occur during times of stress or depression.

Having relationships that are unusually intense and unstable (such as being someone else's ideal, then disliking them severely). Being very uncertain about yourself - not really knowing who they are or what to think about yourself. May be harmful (e.g. money before spending money, risky sexual behavior, use of dangerous drugs or alcohol, reckless driving or eating bananas) or acting indecently.

Repeated self-harm, suicide, or talking and thinking about suicide. Experiencing times of short lived but intense emotional 'low' or irritability or anxiety. This is usually only for a few hours at a time, but sometimes it can last longer. To experience the constant feeling of being 'empty' from within.

Experiencing anger that is exceptionally intense, and in proportion to what triggers anger, and being unable to overcome it (such as having a mood or fighting a fight). When under stress, others may experience extreme doubts or unusual feelings of being separated from their emotions, body or surroundings. There are some explained symptoms of Borderline Personality Disorder that are given below:

Fear of giving up

Unstable Relationships

Blurring or changing your image

Poor Self-treating

Self-Harming

Highly Emotional Swings

Chronic feelings of emptiness

Explosive Temper

Suspicious or out of touch with reality

Fear of giving up

People with BPD often feel abandoned or lonely. Even something unpleasant, such as a loved one arriving home late or going on a weekend, is in dire fear. This can be a drastic attempt to keep the other person close.

You can beg, kiss, start fighting with each other, track your girlfriend's movements, or physically stop this person from leaving. Unfortunately, this behavior has the opposite affect others sending others away.

Unstable relationship

People with BPD have relationships that are severe and short-lived. You may soon be in love, believing that every new person is something that will make you feel healthy, just to be disappointed.

Your relationships look perfect or awesome, without any middle ground. Your loved ones, friends, or family members may feel that they have become emotional as a result of your swinging from ideal to lack of appreciation, anger and hatred.

Blurring or changing your image

When you have BPD, your feeling is usually unstable. Sometimes you can feel good about yourself, but other times you hate yourself, or even think yourself evil.

You can spend money you can't afford, eat, drive carelessly, lift a shop and engage in risky sex, or abuse drugs or alcohol. These dangerous behaviors can help you feel better in the moment, but it can hurt you and those around you.

Self-Harming

Self-harming behavior that also involves suicide threats or attempts. It is common for people with BPD to commit suicidal and deliberate self-harm. Suicidal behavior involves thinking about suicide, making hints or threats of suicide, or actually attempting suicide.

Self-harm involves all other attempts to hurt yourself without the intention of suicide. Common types of self-harm include biting and burning.

Highly Emotional Swings

Unstable feelings and moods are common with BPD. For a moment, you can feel the joy, and the next, the frustration. The little things that other people brush can send you into an emotional tail spin.

These mood swings are severe, but they go away fast (unlike the emotional swings of depression or bipolar disorder), usually lasting only a few minutes or hours.

Chronic feelings of emptiness

People with BPD often talk about being empty, as if there was a hole or a vacuum inside them. This feeling is restless, so you can try to fill the void with drugs, food, or sex. But nothing is really satisfying.

People with BPD often struggle with skeptics or dubious ideas about the purpose of others. When under pressure, you may even lose touch with reality. You may feel foggy, distant, or feel like you're out of your body.

Chapter 3.   Using Mindfulness To Manage Emotions

Overcoming narcissistic abuse is one of the most difficult things you might ever experience. It takes a lot of effort to find the momentum to jump from the pain that has engulfed your life to a better future. The most natural reaction to abuse is pain. Your life is shattered, your heart is broken, you lose everything. But all is not lost. There are solutions for you, effective solutions that will help you get your life back.

Meditation

Narcissistic abuse leaves victims in emotional trauma. The kind of trauma you experience in such a relationship has long-lasting effects on your life. One of the most effective ways of healing, managing and overcoming the negativity you experience from a narcissist is meditation.

Meditation is useful for virtually any condition that is either caused or exacerbated by stress. Meditation helps your body relax, in the process reducing your metabolism rate, improving your heart rate, and reducing your blood pressure (Huntington, 2015). It also helps your brain waves function properly, and helps you breathe better. As you learn how to relax through meditation, the tension in your muscles oozes out of your body from your muscles where tension resides.

The best thing about meditation is that you can perform it even when you have a very busy schedule. You only need a few minutes daily, and you will be on your way to recovery. During meditation, try and focus on your breathing. Listen to the air flowing in and out of your body. This action helps you focus by following the path the air takes in and out of your body. It is one of the easiest ways to calm down.

As the air moves in and out of your body, try and scan your body to identify the areas where tension is high. Observe your thoughts so you are aware of what you are trying to overcome through meditation. It is okay to feel the overwhelming sensations, but do not judge yourself. Recovery is not a sprint. It might take you a few sessions, but your commitment will see you through.

Do not reject your emotions. Your emotions are a part of who you are. It is normal to react in a certain way to someone's actions or behavior towards you. Embrace the feelings and overcome the negativity. Meditation will help you make the neural pathways to and from your brain healthier and stronger by increasing density of grey matter. You learn to be mindful of your feelings and emotions again, and with time, you break the toxic connection you had with your narcissistic abuser.

Trauma and distress affects your brain by disrupting parts of the brain that regulate planning, memory, learning, focus, and emotional regulation. Over the years, meditation has proven a useful technique in overcoming these challenges by improving the function of the hippocampus, amygdala and prefrontal cortex.

As a victim of narcissistic abuse, once your abuser gets control over your life, you have nothing else but to follow their command. However, meditation gets you back in control of your life. You can reclaim your realities, heal and become empowered to overcome all challenges you experienced under their control.

Group therapy

Group therapy is one of the options you can consider when healing from narcissistic abuse. One of the first things you will learn in group therapy is that you cannot fix your narcissistic abuser. However, what you will learn is how to deal with narcissism.

Most of the time victims are encouraged to walk out of such abusive relationships, because there can only be hurt and trauma from them. Narcissists are ruthless in their pursuit of adulation, attention and gratification. They are aware that what they seek is impossible to achieve, so they delude themselves in the idea that they can make you achieve it for them.

Group therapy for narcissistic abuse is helpful because you get one thing you haven't had in a very long time, support. Each time you hear about the experiences of other group members, you realize you are not alone. The overwhelming feelings you have been going through become lighter, because you learn that there are people out there who can relate to what has been eating you inside.

While group therapy has its benefits, you will have to play your part to enjoy these benefits. Your willingness to heal is signified by the fact that you are taking the first step to seek help. Commit to the therapy sessions by taking a pledge of what you want out of it. Once you are in, participate. It might not be easy at first because you have to open up to strangers, but you will get the hang of it. It is okay to sit and listen to others tell their story at first. Once you feel comfortable, you can open up. Remember that it gets easier over time as you keep sharing. Never hold back. Therapy is a safe place. By sharing your experience, you are not just letting the group in on your pain, you might also be helping someone else in the group open up about theirs.

Cognitive behavioral therapy

Cognitive behavioral therapy (CBT) is a therapeutic process that combines cognitive therapy and behavioral therapy to help patients overcome traumatic events that have wielded control away from them. Cognitive therapy focuses on the influence your thoughts and beliefs have in your life, while behavioral therapy is about identifying and changing unhealthy behavioral patterns (Triscari et al, 2015)

CBT is effective because your therapist doesn't just sit down and listen, they also act as your coach. It is a healthy exchange where you learn useful strategies that can help you manage your life better. You learn to recognize your emotional responses, behavior and perceptions.

CBT is ideal for victims of narcissistic abuse because it helps them understand their emotional experiences, identify behavioral patterns, especially problematic tendencies, and learn how to stay in control over some of the most difficult situations in their lives.

Cognitive processing therapy

CPT is a subset of CBT. It is one of the most recommended methods of treating trauma patients. Victims of narcissistic abuse usually go through a lot of trauma, and they can develop PTSD. When you develop PTSD, you might have a different concept of the environment around you, your life and people you interact with. PTSD affects your perception of life in the following areas:

- Safety

After experiencing abuse, you are conditioned to feel unsafe about yourself and everyone else around you. PTSD can exacerbate these fears about safety. You are afraid you cannot take care of yourself, or anyone else.

- Trust

Narcissists break you down to the ground. They make sure you can no longer trust anyone, or yourself. In the aftermath, PTSD can cause you to not trust yourself to make the right call.

- Control

You don't just lose control over your life, you depend on your abuser to guide you through your life. Narcissism does this to you. Narcissists are happy when they have control over your life because it shows them they have your attention and can do anything they please with you. After leaving a narcissist, PTSD can reinforce a feeling of a loss of control, which makes getting back on your feet a very slow process.

- Esteem

One of the painful things about surviving a narcissist is the way they erode your confidence. Even some of the most confident people who have ever lived ended up unable to recognize who they are or what their lives are about anymore. You shy away from situations that require confidence and astute decision making, which you would have embraced willingly earlier on. Your perception of yourself is a broken, unworthy person.

- Intimacy

Among other manipulative tricks narcissists use, triangulation makes you feel so insecure about yourself and intimacy. You feel insecure because no one understands you, and at the same time, you cannot understand why they behave towards you the way they do. Following narcissistic abuse, PTSD may give you moments of flashbacks to the points when your intimacy was insecure. It can make it difficult to start new relationships.

All these thoughts end up in negative emotions clouding your life, like anger, guilt, anxiety, depression, and fear. Through CPT, you learn useful skills that help in challenging these emotions. The negative emotions create a false sense of being that embeds in your subconscious, making you feel like a lesser being. CPT helps by repairing your perception of yourself and the world around you. You learn how to challenge the abuse and gain a better, positive and healthy perspective of your life.

Yoga

For a trauma survivor, yoga can offer an avenue to healing. The restorative benefits of yoga have long been practiced in Eastern traditional societies for wellness. Yoga helps you establish a connection between the mind and your body. It helps you stay grounded. This is one of the things that you need when you survive a narcissistic relationship.

Yoga has been demonstrated in the past to be effective in treating different physical and mental conditions, trauma-related problems, and stress (Criswell, Wheeler, & Partlow Lauttamus, 2014). By combining breathing exercises, physical movement and relaxation, yoga helps you cultivate mindfulness and become more aware of your environment, internal and external.

Breaking up and walking out of a relationship with a narcissist is just the first step. Healing takes more steps. You need to find your bearings. You need to end the confusion that has engulfed your life to the point where you lack an identity.

During yoga, you will focus on breathing exercises. Breathing is one of the most effective and free ways of getting relief. Whether you are going through a difficult period, emotional upheaval or a moment of anxiety, all you have to do is breathe.

Each time you feel the urge to bring the narcissist back into your life, find a comfortable place where you can sit quietly and relax. Close your eyes and breathe. Focus on your breathing, counting your breaths to take your mind away from the problem. Gentle yoga classes can help with this.

Art therapy

Art therapy is founded in the idea that mental well-being and healing can be fostered through creativity. Art is not just a skill, it is also a technique that can be used to help in mental health. Art therapy has been used in psychotherapy for years. Art allows patients to express themselves without necessarily talking to someone about what they feel.

It is ideal for people who struggle to express themselves verbally. Art can help you learn how to communicate better with people, manage stress and even learn more about your personality. Through art therapy, experts believe that their patients can learn how to solve problems, resolve conflicts, ease stress, learn good behavior, develop or sharpen interpersonal skills, and increase their esteem and awareness (Lusebrink, n.d.)

Art therapists have a lot of tools at their disposal that can be used to help you overcome the trauma of a narcissistic relationship. From collages, to sculpture and painting, there is so much to work with. Art therapy is recommended for people who have survived emotional trauma, depression, anxiety, domestic abuse, physical violence and other psychological problems from an abusive relationship with a narcissist.

The difference between an art therapy session and an art class is that in therapy, the emphasis is on your experiences. Your imagination, feelings, and ideas matter. These are things that your narcissist partner might have conditioned you to give up. You will learn some amazing art skills and techniques, but before you do that, your therapist will encourage you to express yourself from deep within. Instead of focusing on what you can see physically, you learn to create things that you imagine or feel.

EMDR

Eye Movement Desensitization and Reprocessing (EMDR) is another technique that you can consider to heal from narcissistic abuse. It is a technique that helps to reprogram your brain away from trauma, so it can learn how to reprocess memories. Exposure to persistent trauma might see your brain form a pattern which perpetuates the negativity you have experienced for a long time (Mosquera & Knipe, 2015)

Traumatic memories cause victims a lot of psychological distress. EMDR is a unique method of treatment because you don't have to talk through your feelings and problems. The brain is instead stimulated to change the emotions you feel, months or even years after you walk away from a narcissist.

EMDR works because the eye movement enables the brain to open up, making it easier to access your memories in a manner that the brain can reprocess in a safe environment other than the environment in which your trauma was perpetuated. After accessing your memories, it is possible to replace them with more empowering feelings and thoughts, so that over time you dissociate from the pain and embrace more fulfilling responses to the triggers in your environment. Flashbacks, nightmares, and anxiety soon become distant memories as you embrace a new life and free yourself from their hold.

For victims of narcissistic abuse, your brain remembers the painful memories of verbal, sexual, psychological, emotional and even physical abuse. In an EMDR session, you are encouraged to focus on the details of any such traumatic events, while at the same time viewing something else for a short time.

What happens is that while you focus on both the negative memories and a new positive affirmation, your memory feels different. You will also learn self-soothing techniques to help you continue dissociating from the pain. EMDR helps to unchain the shackles in your life and allow your brain to think about experiences differently.

Self-hypnosis

Hypnotherapy has been used successfully to help victims of narcissistic abuse heal for so many years. There are specific conditions that must be met however, for this to work. You must ensure you are in the presence of specific stimuli that can encourage hypnosis. You will also learn how to narrow down your focus and awareness, and finally, allow yourself to freely experience your feelings without making a conscious choice to do so.

Narcissists are not capable of genuine connection, but instead they project their feelings and insecurities about loneliness and abandonment to their victim. How do you get into a trance state for hypnosis? Emotional abuse has a significant impact on your life. Hypnosis allows you to relax effortlessly. Effortless relaxation is one of the last things you might have experienced throughout your ordeal with a narcissist. The moment you are capable of allowing yourself to relax without struggling, you open doors to healing your mind and your body.

Self-hypnosis is a transformative process that restores your belief in yourself, encourages you to learn important emotional tools that can help you recover from abuse, and also help to protect yourself in the future. With each session, you become stronger, and calm. The waves of emotional upheaval you used to experience reduce and you become at peace with yourself and your environment.

Self-hypnosis also gives you a clearer picture of what your life is about. You let go of the negative vibes and embrace peace. You are set on a path to rediscovery. You find more value in yourself than you ever had throughout your narcissistic relationship. As you go on with these sessions, you learn how to take the necessary steps towards healing, and moving in the right direction in life. The most important thing behind self-hypnosis is that you start looking forward to a new life, and you actually believe in your ability to succeed while at it.

Aromatherapy

Even though it might feel like you are at the edge of a cliff and there is no way back for you, it is possible to recover from narcissistic abuse. Many people have done it before and you can do it too. Recovery from this kind of trauma is very sweet. Each time you make progress, you can look back at how far gone you were, and the changes you have made. It helps you appreciate your life, and realize how toxic it was earlier on.

Aromatherapy is one of the conscious efforts you take towards healing and recovering from narcissistic abuse. Think about aromatherapy in the same way you think about exercise. If you feel you are unfit, you exercise regularly. You can schedule three or four training sessions weekly to help you stay in shape.

The same applies to aromatherapy. Narcissists leave you so unfit emotionally. You need to get your emotions in shape so that you can live a happy and fulfilling life. To free yourself of emotional distress, you need to stimulate your amygdala. Smell is one of the best ways to stimulate the amygdala. There is a strong connection between your emotions and sense of smell, a connection that has been there since you were a child.

The sense of smell is closely associated with emotional connections, whether positive or negative. This explains why each time you smell your favorite food being prepared, it reminds you of an event during which you enjoyed it. Smell, therefore, helps to induce comfort, and nostalgia. If smells can take you way back, it can also help to remind

44

you of the traumatic events that you suffered through narcissistic abuse.

Chapter 4. Epidemiology, Factors Of Borderline Personality Disorder

The co-existence of intense varied moods such as impulsive anger, mania and depression that characterize borderline personality disorder was accounted by Hippocrates and Homer. The term was revived during the late 1600s by Swiss physician Theophile Bonet and he described the phenomenon of having unstable emotions followed by unpredictability. However, the term "borderline" was coined in 1938 by Adolf Stern as he described a group of patients who suffered from what he thought was mild schizophrenia and borderline of psychosis and neurosis. Because patients exhibited borderline symptoms of such conditions, thus the condition was named as such.

About 35% of people who suffer from borderline personality disorder experience remission from their treatment. With long-term treatment, several studies noted that more than 86% of people who suffer from borderline personality disorder can achieve stable recovery. Contrary to what most people believe in, patients who suffer from borderline personality disorder can recover even from their severe symptoms.

Epidemiology

The prevalence of borderline personality disorder occurs at 1% to 2% of the general population. Moreover, women are also more likely to suffer from borderline personality disorder than men because of the surplus of hormone estrogen. In a 2008 study, it was found out that borderline personality disorder is more likely to occur at 5.6% in men and 6.2% in women. However, the percentage of occurrence for borderline personality disorder is negligible according to some experts.

This particular personality disorder is estimated to contribute at least 20% of all cases in psychiatric admission. Moreover, this condition also accounts for 10% of outpatient psychiatric consultation in the United States.

On the other hand, the borderline personality disorder is also a common condition that has afflicted inmates all over the country. The overall prevalence of borderline personality disorder in prison population in the United States is 17%. The high number of prevalence in US prison is related to the high frequency of prisoners involved in substance abuse and mood disorders.

As mentioned earlier, people who suffer from borderline personality disorder can recover from their condition. However, the recovery can be staggering because of the burst of emotions coming from the patient. Although this may be the case, people suffering from this condition can still live normal healthy lives. Below are treatment and management options available for people suffering from borderline personality disorder.

Psychotherapy

Psychotherapy is the most common method to treat people suffering from borderline personality disorder. Treatments are often based on the needs of the patient. Patients suffering from borderline personality disorder needs to undergo long-term psychotherapy in order to have better chances of coping from their condition. There are different types of treatments for psychotherapy that patients can undergo and below is a discussion of the different types of psychotherapy treatments available to patients suffering from this disorder.

Mentalization-based treatment: This is a type of psychodynamic psychotherapy. It is specifically designed for people suffering from borderline personality disorder. The focus of this treatment is to place enhancements to the patient by allowing them to recover mentalization so that the psychotherapist can work with the current mental state of the patient. This procedure is usually done as individual or group therapy. This particular method aims to encourage the patient to develop attachment to their peers.

Transference-focused psychotherapy: This type of psychotherapy method is done in a twice-weekly manner. It is highly structured and was developed specifically for patients suffering from borderline personality disorder. The aim of this psychotherapy method is to reduce the self-injurious behavior of patients.

Dialectical behavior therapy: This particular psychotherapy method aims to reduce the risk of self-harm, suicidal behavior and substance abuse of patients suffering from mental disorders.

General psychiatric management: This particular psychotherapy treatment strategy is an evidence-based treatment approach in treating mental disorders. Treatment procedures used in general psychiatric management include cognitive behavioral therapy and psychoanalytic object relations therapy.

Schema-focused therapy: The schema therapy is an integrative way of treating a wide spectrum of mental and character-logical problems such as borderline personality disorder. It combines techniques and theories such as cognitive behavioral therapy, attachment therapy and psychoanalytic object relations theory in treating patients.

The efficacy of the psychotherapy treatment options depends largely on the patients. However, studies indicate that mentalization-based therapy and dialectical behavior therapy are both effective in treating all subtypes of borderline personality disorder.

The problem, however, with psychotherapy is that it is a long-term treatment that can put a huge financial strain on the patient and his or her immediate family. Funding a long-term psychotherapy session for patients suffering from borderline personality disorder is very expensive but many researchers are now developing shorter versions of the treatment options to increase the availability of the treatment to as many people as possible.

However, the cost of the psychotherapy is not the only thing that makes this treatment option challenging. Since patients suffering from this condition fear rejection, psychotherapists need to be flexible when it comes to dealing with the negative attributions of the patient.

Meditation

Research indicates that meditation can also bring favorable changes in the brain of patients suffering from borderline personality disorder. Meditation can also bring improvement to the symptoms that characterize the borderline personality disorder. In fact, many psychiatrists recommend meditation as adjunct treatment of psychotherapy.

Outpatient and Inpatient Admissions

Majority of patients who suffer from borderline personality disorder have better chances of improving if they go to outpatient or inpatient admissions. There are many facilities all over the country that cater to full-time care of people suffering from different kinds of mental disorders including borderline personality disorder. However, the problem with this type of management option is that it is very expensive thus only a few individuals can afford to get treatment from these facilities.

So which treatment option should a person suffering from borderline personality disorder opt for? There is no definite answer and it is important to encourage a borderline individual to see a psychiatrist who will design the appropriate treatment to manage the condition of the patient.

Moderating Factors in Treating Borderline Personality Disorder

Just like the other types of personality disorders, there are moderating factors that can affect the efficacy of treatment options for patients suffering from borderline personality disorder. This section will deal with the different factors that influence the efficacy of treatments as well as recovery of the patients suffering from this condition.

Executive Function

The executive function refers to the brain faculties of people. It is how we react to different stimuli thrown at us. The executive functions among people who suffer from borderline personality disorder mediate the relationship between its symptoms and sensitivity towards rejection. This means that the symptoms largely affect the cognitive processes of the brain. For instance, the brain dictates a person with borderline personality disorder to act more on his or her impulse and this also affects the efficacy of treatment that a patient undergoes.

Family Environment

The immediate family environment also mediates the development as well as the recovery of a patient suffering from borderline personality disorder.

Self-Complexity

A patient suffering from borderline personality disorder has a lot of characteristics and experiences a wide variety of emotions at one time.

This self-complexity makes it very difficult for psychiatrists to treat people with borderline disorder. The thing is that patients who have this condition suffer an inner battle full of ironies that it is difficult to help them realize that they should only have a linear track for their emotions.

Suppression of Thoughts

Though suppression is a common defense mechanism of people suffering from borderline personality disorder, it is the intentional attempt to avoid thinking certain thoughts that might make people suffers vulnerability. Thought suppression makes patients with borderline personality disorder more secretive and recalcitrant to treatment.

The borderline personality disorder may be one of the personality disorders that are very easy to spot but it certainly is also one of the most difficult to treat because patients are aware of their condition yet they are very stubborn to accept change. Nevertheless, it is still possible to help them recover through constant therapy and patience.

Chapter 5.   Diagnosis Of The Disorder

One of the hardest things to do with this kind of disorder is to diagnose it. Most of the people who have it are not going to want to have anything to do with the doctor or psychiatrist who is trying to help them out and so they are going to ignore them and not take the help. Often it is going to take family members to see the issue and initiate the help that is needed before the person with the disorder is going to get the help. They are not going to go in on their own because they are not going to see that they have any issues at all.

Once you can get the person with the disorder to come into the door, the diagnosis of this disorder is going to be based on the assessment that is done in the clinic by a professional of mental health. The best way to do this is to present the different criteria of the disorder to the patient, these criteria are listed above, and ask them if they think that any of these describe them. This is going to get the participant involved in the cure, making it more likely to work. Plus, a doctor is usually not going to have enough time or outside experience with the patient to determine on their own if the characteristics are there and this can provide them with a usually truthful means of getting to it.

When you allow the person who has this kind of disorder to actively help with the diagnosis, they are going to be more willing to get the help that the professional is going to get them. There are some clinicians though who decide that it is best to not tell their patients that they have this diagnosis because they believe that it is full of stigma and the person will be against the treatment because they may have heard in the past that this is an untreatable disorder. While this is one way to go, there is a lot of research to show that the person suffering from the disease should know about it to get the most effective treatment that is possible.

During this evaluation, the patient is going to be asked a lot of questions about their symptoms including when they began and how severe they were. The might also be asked some questions that relate to how these symptoms are impacting their life. Some of the issues that the doctor is going to take special notes about would be any thoughts that are about harming others, experiences with doing self-harm, and any thoughts of suicide that the person has.

The diagnosis is going to be based on what the patient has been reporting at sessions as well as what the doctor has been able to observe in their short time. These two things are usually going to be able to combine to give a good outlook on what is going on. There are a few other tests that can be done to help determine if borderline personality disorder is present in the person. Sometimes some laboratory tests or a physical exam are going to be done to help rule out some of the other things that might trigger these symptoms, such as the person abusing substances or a thyroid condition; both of which could cause some of the same behaviors as what is find in borderline personality disorder.

Once the disorder has been determined and diagnosed in a patient, it is time to get to work with giving them the treatment that they need to stay healthy and get their lives back. While this is going to be a lot of work and will take some time, it is something that must be done if the person wants to get their life back and be much happier. Here is some more information about how the disorder could be diagnosed and how the person should get the help that they need to start feeling better in no time.

International Classifications

There are a few classifications that you will be able to find that are used internationally to help make the diagnosis. These classifications can be nice because they allow the clinician to be able to do the diagnosis without having to go on their own personal beliefs and can keep everything organized and the same throughout. The idea of borderline personality disorder, is one that is recognized by the World Health Organization

Impulsive Type

The first kind of category that is recognized in this is the impulsive type. Out of the things that are discussed below, at least three of them need to be present to diagnose someone with this category of the disorder.

A marked tendency to get out of control or to act out. This is going to happen unexpectedly and will not be due to someone causing the issue or forcing them to act out. Often the act is going to be done by the person without them worrying or even thinking about the consequences that could happen with their action. This is just something that they are going to do, perhaps over a slight disagreement or other issue, that should not have been that big of a deal but which was turned into one.

A marked tendency of the sufferer to get into behavior that is considered quarrelsome and they are going to have a lot of conflicts with the others around them. This is especially going to be true with impulsive acts that have been criticized or thwarted. This is a person who is routinely getting into fights with others around them and who see any little slight as an excuse to get in a big fight together.

A liability to having strong outbursts when it comes to violence or anger. Not only are they having these issues, but they do not have the ability that is needed to control the explosions or other issues that come up. They will seem very angry but they will also seem like they do not have the means to come back down and be calm again even if they had wanted.

These people are also going to have some difficulty in staying with their course of action if they are not able to get a reward right away. They may have been really interested in doing it, but when it did not provide the immediate reward that they were looking for, they most likely became upset and angry and so decided to just give up on it. This is something that would happen quite often and the person would only stick with things they know they can finish and be rewarded with.

These people will often have capricious and unstable moods that can change almost without any warning. It might be hard to keep up with these kinds of people.

These are the five criteria that will often be found in someone who is dealing with the impulsive kind of this disorder. You are going to notice that they are going to do things often without any thought to what they are doing or what is going to happen when they are done, and this can be a dangerous thing. For a person to be diagnosed with this kind of disorder, they are going to need to have at least three of the things mentioned above present when they talk to their therapist in the office.

Borderline Type

Next comes the borderline type. This one is going to be a little bit different. This is going to take a bit from the list above and then adds in a bit from the list that is going to be presented below. You will need to have a minimum of three of those symptoms that are found for the impulsive type present as well as a minimum of 2 of the ones below to get a diagnosis of this category. Some of the things to look for include:

A person with this type would often have some uncertainty and disturbances in their self-image as well as their internal preferences and their aims in life. They do not think that they are worth much and even though they crave interaction with others, they are not sure why these others would want to have anything to do with them. They may wonder around a lot looking confused because they do not know who they are, what they should do with their lives, or what is to become of them.

They might also have a higher liability to get involved in relationships that are often unstable and intense. This might include those whirlwind relationships where they meet and get married in just a few short months, but it does not have to be this severe either to fit. Since the relationship is so unstable it is not going to last and since it was intense, it is likely to cause a sort of emotional crisis in the person who is suffering from the disorder.

These people are going to show really excessive efforts to never become abandoned. They are scared that one day they will wake up and not have anyone around to be their friends or to help them out when they need. This is further complicated by the fact that they are pushing others away and are not very good at seeing other's points of view. They are going to work almost obsessively to make sure that others do not leave them alone so that they can always have the help and companionship that they are looking for.

They are also going to have frequent threats as well as acts of self-harm. This is often not in an attempt to get someone to act the way that they would like or to change the feelings of someone else. This is more of something that they do in the hopes of getting their own emotions in check. They are going to have a lot of trouble with their own emotions and since they are not able to keep them under control, they may turn to self-harm in the hopes of getting some relief.

Frequent feelings that surround them of emptiness. Because they do not have any plans for their future or for the things that they want to do in their lives, they are going to feel empty. They do not have any goals or long term plans, so often they are just going to wander around and hope that things work out the best. This can lead to a life that is pretty empty.

They are going to often demonstrate behavior that is impulsive. This is going to include things such as substance abuse and speeding. The idea behind doing these things is because it gives the sufferer a bit of a break for the bad feelings or uncontrolled emotions that they are going through so that they can just feel better for a bit. The issue comes when the person begins to feel a bit guilty about their behavior and so they will feel even worse than they did before. As mentioned before, there needs to be quite a few things that are present before someone is going to be diagnosed with this form of the disorder. But those who meet these requirements should get the help that they need as soon as possible.

Family Members

Even the way that the person with the disorder is treating the others who are around them can be a way of diagnosing them. People who have this disorder are going to be much more prone to disliking their family members and they are often going to be angry at these same people. Often the person with the disorder is going to work to alienate themselves from the family because they are mad over some little slight or they are worried that the family members are going to become to see a problem. Often the family members are going to feel a bit helpless and angry about the way that they are relating with this person and may wonder what they can do to make things right again.

There was a study done in 2003 that found that the thoughts of the family members would change once they found out that the behavior was for a reason. In most cases, the anger and hurt towards the person with the disorder would go up once their family members began to understand what is going on. While this would not seem like something that would happen, it is often believed that these feelings are occurring because the family is being given the wrong kind of information about the disorder so they are blaming the person rather than the issue at hand.

The best way for family members to be able to help out the one that they love is to learn as much as possible about the disorder. It is easy to start looking through books and watching shows about the disorder and while this might be a good place to start in some cases, you will find that it is often the wrong information. Get out there and find the information that is the right information and this is going to help make more sense out of what you are seeing with your loved one.

This is going to be just as difficult for members of the family to handle as it is for the person who is going through the issue. They are the ones who have been emotionally harmed by their loved one not wanting to have anything to do with them. It is important that the family gets the therapy and help that they need to feel better about the situation. Understanding the whole situation and how it is affecting the family and the sufferer can make it easier to get through the whole situation together.

Diagnosing with Other Disorders

It is not uncommon for someone who is dealing with this kind of disorder to also have some other disorders, whether it is other personality disorders or something else, that are going to show up at the same time. This makes it even harder to find the personality disorder because it may be masked by some of the other symptoms that are there. Compared to those who have some of the other personality disorders, those who have borderline personality disorder are going to have a higher rate for also meeting the criteria for other disorders such as:

Mood disorders—this is going to include things like bipolar disorder and major depression

Anxiety disorders—there are a lot of these that can be met as well and would include post-traumatic stress disorder, social anxiety disorder, and panic disorder
Other kinds of personality disorder
Substance abuse
Eating disorders—this would include things like bulimia and anorexia nervosa
Attention deficit hyperactivity disorder
Somatoform disorders
Dissociative disorders

If a person with this personality disorder has one of these other issues, they should not be diagnosed with the personality disorder until that other issue has been dealt with. These other issues can give some of the same symptoms and sometimes taking care of these can be a simpler method of dealing with the personality disorder. This is unless the symptoms of the personality disorder can be proven to have been around for many years before the other issue came into play.

Also, it is more likely that women are going to experience some of the issues listed above while men will receive some of the others. For example, men are going to be higher with the substance use disorders while the women are going to have more of the eating disorders. It is important that you get these other disorders taken care of if you would like to see some of the best results with treating your borderline personality disorder. It is going to be pretty much impossible to take care of the personality disorder if you have some of the other issues listed above in the way because these are going to onset the disorder and will keep it going even with a lot of therapy in the process.

This is why most professionals will do a thorough examination of the patient to figure out if there are some other issues that are present in the patient. This can make it much easier to cure the personality disorder once the other issues are done. This can be done with some preliminary therapy or through the use of medications to treat issues such as like anxiety and depression for the best results.

Chapter 6.   Treatment And Medication

Each person's experience with borderline personality disorder is different. Some symptoms may be more dominant; while for one he could be more paranoid, for another he would be more dissociative. Depending on the situation and circumstances, a therapist can recommend the right treatment for borderline personality disorder.

When one has BPD it can oftentimes be a scary experience that leaves one feeling isolated because it causes a strain on relationships. Individuals with BPD need the guidance of therapists to overcome this aspect of the disorder so that they can go back to their normal life and benefit from the joy that healthy human relationships can bring. Treatment for BPD can provide people with valuable skills that they need to carry out into the world for maintaining interpersonal relationships. Additionally, treatment can reduce the stress involved through the prescription of medication that decreases BPD symptoms.

Psychotherapy

Psychotherapy is the most common treatment of choice for people with mental illnesses especially those who have BPD. Although there are many forms of psychotherapy, they all have one goal in common and that is to help patients better understand the way their thoughts and emotions operate. It is an important aspect of treatment because while medication can help reduce certain symptoms of borderline personality disorder, it will not teach patients how to learn coping skills or regulate emotions the way psychotherapy does.

Psychotherapy is also crucial in helping people refrain from committing suicide. This is why therapists and other medical professionals involved stay in touch with the patient, constantly evaluating their vulnerability to suicide throughout the entire treatment. When a patient has severe feelings of suicide, hospitalization is the next step.

Dialectical Behavior Therapy

The most famous and effective form of psychotherapy known today is Dialectical Behavior Therapy or DBT. It was founded by Marsha Linehan, and is a program that teaches people how to take better control of their lives and emotions. DBT also has a strong focus on emotion regulation, self-knowledge, and cognitive restructuring. DBT has a comprehensive approach and is usually conducted with a group. However, the skill set taught through Dialectical Behavior Therapy is considered complex and therefore not recommended to people who have difficulty learning new concepts.

Dialectical Behavior Therapy utilizes two concepts: validation and dialectics. In validation, the client is taught to accept that their emotions are real, acceptable, and valid. On the other hand, dialectics is a form of philosophy which teaches that life is not to be seen as black and white. It also reinforces the importance of accepting ideas even though they are contradicting to one's own beliefs.

Therapists specializing in DBT work with those who are prone to suicide by engaging them in mindfulness, interpersonal effectiveness, emotion regulation, and distress tolerance. When people with BPD learn that there are healthy ways of coping and handling one's emotions, the risk of them committing self-harm and suicide are significantly decreased.

Borderline personality disorder, just like other personality disorders, is challenging to treat. Because the goal of treatment is to change the way a person views the world, stress, and other people, treatment is usually lengthy. Treatment for BPD is usually at least a year but can go on for much longer.

There are also other forms of psychotherapy that are used to address borderline personality disorder that focus on conflict resolution and social learning theory. These are more solution-focused therapies which fail to address the core issue of people who suffer from BPD which is difficulty regulating their emotions.

Schema Focused Therapy

Schema Focused Therapy is a type of psychotherapy whose primary goal is to identify and treat unhealthy ways of thinking. Some elements of schema focused therapy include elements that are also found in cognitive behavioral therapy (CBT) and combines it with other methods of psychotherapy.

Schema focused therapy is founded on the principle that if a person's basic childhood needs such as love, acceptance, and a desire for safety are inadequate, this results in the development of unhealthy ways of thinking about the world. These are referred to as maladaptive early schemas. Schemes are defined as broad patterns of behavior and thinking. They are more than simply beliefs because they are closely held patterns that affect the way one perceives and interacts with the world.

The schema theory suggests that schemas occur when events in one's present life bear a resemblance to events in the past that are directly related to the creation of the schema. When a person has unhealthy schemas as a result of a difficult childhood, they will end up developing unhealthy ways of thinking as a response to the situation. Furthermore, schema theory suggests that the symptoms of borderline personality disorder are usually caused by a difficult childhood wherein a child may have experienced abandonment, trauma, or maltreatment by one or both parents, resulting to the development of maladaptive early schemas.

Schema focused therapy for borderline personality disorder seeks to identify relevant schemas in a person's life, and tie them to schemas present in past events. A therapist works to help the patient process the emotional response that arise due to the schema. They then work on addressing unhealthy coping methods to help the patient respond to the scheme in a healthy manner. Schema focused therapy may involve exercises that are designed to halt unhealthy behavioral patterns, change the way one thinks, and encouraging the patient to vent out their anger.

Transference Focused Therapy

Transference Focused Therapy utilizes the patient-therapist relationship in order to improve how a person with borderline personality disorder sees the world. Transference is defined as the process wherein emotions are transferred from one person to the other. It is a key principle used in psychodynamic therapies where it is suggested that the way a client feels about persons that are important in their lives are transferred to his therapist. Through transference therapy, the therapist can clearly understand how the patient interacts with the people in his life in order to help them learn to effectively manage relationships. Eventually, the goal of transference focused therapy is to help patients enjoy having stable relationships again.

Therapists of transference focused therapy believe that symptoms of borderline personality disorder that arise from dysfunctional relationships one experienced during childhood continue in adulthood, thereby damaging the ability of these adults to have normal, healthy relationships. The interactions we have with our primary caregivers during childhood contributes to how we develop a sense of self and also affects how we perceive other people. If one does not have a healthy relationship with their caregivers during childhood, this results in adults having difficulty relating to other people and having a good sense of oneself.

Evidence shows that maltreatment or trauma or loss of caregivers during childhood increases one's risk in developing borderline personality disorder. And because these symptoms have a negative impact, preventing one from developing relationships with people later on, some experts on BPD agree that it is important to address this by helping people focus on improving relationships through transference focused therapy.

With this kind of therapy there is a focus on the relationship between the patient and the therapist. Unlike other forms of therapy where the therapist provides instructions on what the patient should do, transference focused therapy involves asking the client numerous questions during the discussion while they explore reactions. Furthermore, there is added emphasis on events that happen in the present moment instead of seeking out past experiences. For example, instead of spending time discussing issues with caregivers during one's childhood, the discussion is focused on how the client relates to their own therapist.

Therapists who practice transference based therapy are also skilled at remaining neutral, which is a reason why this kind of treatment is effective. They know not to give their opinion on their patient's reaction, and will also not be available outside session hours except for emergencies.

Mentalization-Based Therapy

Mentalization-based therapy (MBT) is another form of psychotherapy. MBT is based on the premise that people who have borderline personality disorder have difficulty thinking about their own thoughts. This means that people with BPD are unable to examine their own thoughts, beliefs, opinions, and if they are realistic and useful to them. An example of this is when individuals with BPD may have sudden urges to harm themselves and end up giving in without thinking about the consequences of their actions.

MBT is also important because it helps people realize that others have their own thoughts and beliefs, and your own interpretation of their mental states is not always correct. Additionally, it helps people realize that actions will have an impact on other people's mentality. The main goal of MBT is to help clients recognize their own as well as others' mental states. It also teaches people with BPD how to step back from their own thoughts and examine if they are valid first. MBT may be conducted within a hospital as a form of inpatient therapy. Treatment is composed of daily sessions with a therapist as well as group sessions.

MBT usually lasts around 18 months, but depending on the need some patients may be asked to be an inpatient for the entire duration of their treatment. Some hospitals and treatment facilities will allow patients to leave at specified times during the course of their treatment.

Therapeutic Communities

Therapeutic Communities (TC) is a form of psychotherapy wherein people with various psychological conditions interact in a structured environment. This kind of treatment is best suited for those who have issues dealing with emotions and who are suicidal. By teaching them the skills needed for healthy social interaction with a wide range of people, people with borderline personality disorder can better cope with their problems. TC therapy is usually residential and held in houses where clients stay 1-4 days a week.

Apart from individual and group sessions involved in TC, it also requires patients to participate in other activities designed to improve one's social skills and boost confidence. These activities include doing household chores, prepare and cook meals, play games, and participate in recreational activities. Therapeutic communities also involve all participants in regular community meetings where people with different psychological conditions meet in order to discuss issues and concerns within the community.

One of the unique features of the therapeutic community method of treatment is that it is run democratically. All members, including staff, can contribute their opinion on how TC's should be run. In fact, they can even vote if they think an individual should or shouldn't be admitted within the community. This means that even if one's therapist thinks that a therapeutic community is the best form of treatment for a case of borderline personality disorder, it doesn't mean that they will automatically be granted entry. Guidelines for acceptable behavior are defined in each TC because they set restrictions such as the prohibition of alcohol consumption, violence towards one self and other members of the community. Members who break the guidelines may be asked to leave the TC.

Although a therapeutic community is one of the widely accepted methods of treatment for people with borderline personality disorder, there is insufficient evidence to tell if a TC is effective for everyone. This is particularly the case for people with BPD who have difficulty following rules since TC's can be quite strict with guidelines.

Self-Care

Over the course of treatment, patients are usually given a telephone number that they can call if they think they are undergoing a severe crisis. It could occur when people with BPD are experiencing episodes of extreme symptoms and are more prone to self-harm and suicide. A number may be directed to the community mental health care practitioners, social workers, or other medical professionals. Depending on the area, a crisis resolution team service may also be available since they specialize in caring for people with serious mental health issues. Oftentimes these teams come to the rescue of individuals who may require hospitalization because of suicide attempts.

Those who suffer from borderline personality disorder usually find that merely talking to someone about what they are going through can help them get out of their crisis. Certain cases, although rare, may require medication such as tranquilizers to calm one's mood. Medications such as these are usually prescribed for 7 days to stabilize emotions.

Individuals with borderline personality disorder are encouraged to attend support groups for social support from those who are going through the same experience as they are. Support groups are useful in providing moral support through sharing common thoughts and feelings. Patients can also try coping skills and learn how to regulate their emotions with friends they make at these support groups. They have proven to be a crucial part of helping people with BPD expand their skill set while developing healthy social relationships and eventually reduce their symptoms in the long run.

If you are the one suffering from borderline personality disorder, you may also find it challenging to take better care of yourself. However, those who are diagnosed with BPD should make it a priority to take better care of themselves because the symptoms may be exacerbated when one neglects self-care.

The basics of self-care involve engaging in activities that promote relaxation and good health. This means getting enough exercise, good sleep, taking the medications as prescribed by your therapist, eating nutritious food, and dealing with stress in healthy ways. People who take good care of themselves are less prone to suffering from psychiatric

illnesses which is why self-care is necessary for everyone. It is especially important in those who are suffering from BPD because while it can not only worsen the symptoms, it can also result in slower recovery.

Many people tend to underestimate the importance of good sleep when it comes to proper self-care.

Medication

Some doctors agree that medication is useful in the treatment of people with borderline personality disorder but others disagree. Today, there is still no medication that is licensed for the treatment of BPD.

However, some forms of medicine have proven useful in reducing symptoms in certain people.

Usually, selective serotonin reuptake inhibitors (SSRI) are by default the first kind of medication that is prescribed to patients. SSRI's are designed to reduce impulsivity, depression, anger, suicidal behavior, and anxiety in people who suffer from mental health problems.

Medications such as anti-depressants and anti-anxiety pills may be useful to reduce symptoms especially during a crisis or emergency. The most common kinds of antidepressants prescribed for patients of borderline personality disorder include Prozac, Zoloft, Nardil, Wellbutrin, and Effexor. However, this kind of medication is not encouraged for long-term use particularly because depression and anxiety are often short-term symptoms that may come and go as a result of various stressors in a person's life.

Antipsychotics also have a positive effect on patients even though they don't suffer from BPD. These are effective in reducing paranoia, anxiety, hostility, anger, as well as impulsivity in people with borderline personality disorder. Common antipsychotic medications include Haldol, Clozaril, Risperdal, Seroquel, and Zyprexa.

Mood stabilizers are another form of medication that is used to treat symptoms of borderline personality disorder. These are effective in treating impulsivity, mood swings, and the intense changes in emotions caused by BPD. Common types of mood stabilizers include Lithobid, Depakote, Tegretol, and Lamictal.

Medication that specializes in reducing anxiety are known as anxiolytics, and are also prescribed for BPD. While anxiolytics are given to patients of borderline personality disorder, there is still insufficient evidence on the effectiveness of these medications in treating BPD as a whole. In fact, there have been cases where certain types of anxiolytics, known as benzodiazepines, were shown to increase the symptoms of BPD in other people. Common types of anxiolytics used for BPD patients include Valium, Xanax, Ativan, Klonopin, and Buspar.

Before accepting medications from a physician, it is necessary to discuss any side effects thoroughly. If the side effects seem harmful, other forms of medicine may be considered especially if it is clear that the side effects are greater than the benefits. Medication used for borderline personality disorder may vary depending on the kind of medicine. Some of the common side effects are detailed below:

Antidepressants:

Headache

Insomnia

Reduced appetite

Sedation

Sexual dysfunction

Weight gain

Mood stabilizers:

Acne

Tremors

Weight gain

Gastrointestinal distress

Antipsychotics:

Akathisia

Dry mouth

Weight gain

Sexual dysfunction

Sedation

Anti-anxiety:

Fatigue

Sleepiness

Mental slowness

Memory problems

Impaired coordination

How To Know If A Medication Is Working

When you start to take medication for borderline personality disorder, this will result in both emotional and physical changes. If a medication is working well, the first thing that you may notice is a positive change in the way you respond to situations. Although the change is usually gradual and subtle, people experience the benefits of medications in a different time frame from other people. In fact, the positive changes are usually not felt unless they have been happening for some time. It is also common for other people to

notice the changes in your emotional response before you do, so you may want to ask people that you are usually with if they notice any changes.

Chapter 7.   Practicing Mindfulness

There's no way that you could learn a new skill without any form of guidance or instruction. Imagine you're given the keys to a Ferrari, and you're asked to drive it in really heavy traffic, but you've never driven a day in your life. That would not work out well. The same thing applies when it comes to mindfulness. If it were simply a matter of telling you, "Go forth and be mindful," then I had better wrap up this book here because there's nothing else to do, I guess. Don't worry. I'm not going to leave you hanging.

At the core of Dialectical Behavioral Therapy is mindfulness. What we're going to do is take a look at each of the steps you need to go through to practice mindfulness. It's not enough to know it can help you. I want to empower you with the knowledge you need to save yourself.

Now, you may be a tad skeptical of all of this. Perhaps more than a few times already, you have considered setting this book aside, because you find it inconceivable that simply learning mindfulness as a skill could be all you need to turn your life around. It's not unusual for BPD patients to be skeptical of the whole thing. For a problem as complex as BPD, how could anyone possibly even suggest something as simple and basic as mindfulness? What the heck does "mindfulness" even mean anyway? Full of mind? You're tempted to assume it's some religious hokey by Buddhists, and so you should not pay it any attention. There is no way all your problems could be resolved by simply breathing, you think. These are all logical thoughts.

It's natural to raise a brow in suspicion at the whole concept, especially when you have no idea what it really means to practice mindfulness, or how you would even begin in the first place.

Once you know what to do, it becomes easier for you to accept the idea. However, knowledge is not enough. Knowledge is not power. It's the application of the knowledge that will give you all the healing you seek. Just because you know the mechanics do not mean you really know how to work it. The only way to truly know is to practice what you do know. By practice, I do not mean you should try it once or twice. I mean, you should dedicate yourself to being consistent about your mindfulness practice. This is the only way you can truly reap the benefits and get better. It's not unlike working out. You don't expect one day at the gym to undo years of terrible dieting and a lazy lifestyle. You have to keep going regularly. You need to keep training the same muscles over and over again until they get better and stronger. To keep said muscles, you'll need to make working out a lifestyle. The same applies to mindfulness.

Most people who have BPD tend to resort to stopgap measures like cutting, reckless behavior, and other things like that. The problem is these measures are beyond ineffective in the long run. The relief you get in the moment is short-lived, and sooner or later, you will do yourself or some other person irreparable harm. What's the alternative then? Mindfulness. In the practice of mindfulness, you will find long-lasting peace and calm. You will find a more effective solution that can serve you at all times. It will take a bit of time and practice, and you will need to be patient, but in the end, it will pay off.

Laying The Groundwork

You're probably trying to figure out how often and for how long each time you should practice being mindful. Since you're only just starting out, it's best for you to begin with just 15 to 20 minutes a day. You can easily split that up into two sessions, once at the start of your day, and once at the end.

As you get used to your practice, you could begin to add on a bit of time to your sessions each day. We're going to cover ways in which you can be mindful all through your day, but we're also going to cover the basics on picking a set time each day for a more focused, formal session. This is important because being deliberate about it is the only way you can get better at being mindful. One more thing I ought to mention is that no matter how good you become at being mindful, you must make sure you keep up your practice day after day.

This is not a prerequisite. Find a time that is convenient for you and commit to it. If you find that you're exhausted at the end of your day, then you definitely would be better off practicing in the afternoon or in the morning. If you have to start your mornings early and have a lot to do to prepare your family for the day, then you might want to consider noon or night for practice. It's all up to you. The point is you must make it a habit, and remember, the only way habits are formed by constant repetition. Do what you need to in order to make it happen. Leave yourself a note somewhere you'll always pass by, so you can remember, or set a reminder on your phone.

For a lot of people, it helps to practice mindfulness in a certain spot every time. Like I already mentioned, you don't absolutely have to, but it does help to have a sacred space for it. Eventually, though, you will be able to practice mindfulness wherever you find yourself.

Another question that plagues those who are new to mindfulness is what pose or posture they should adopt. Should they sit or stand or something? There are a number of different mindfulness practices. For some of them, you will need to be seated, and for others, you will have to move about a bit. You do not necessarily have to adopt the lotus position if you find that a little tough on your knees.

If it's a seated mindfulness practice, then it would be best to adopt a posture where your chest is open, meaning you keep your arms away from your chest. You also want to make sure that your bottom is firmly and evenly planted on the seat. Choose a good chai, which allows you to sit up comfortably. If you need a few pillows to support your back, then use them. Make sure your feet are flat on the floor, firmly and evenly. Do not cross your ankles or your legs. Your shoulders must be back and upright. Don't hunch over. You may keep your arms on your lap. If you like, you can turn your palms upwards. A huge part of this mindfulness practice is also aware of your posture as you sit. Now that you know how to sit, you're going to practice while keeping your eyes open.

Owning Your Mind

The more you practice mindfulness, the more you'll find that you own your mind. You are more in control of it. Right now, I can see how you'd think this is an impossible feat. However, it's true! As you practice, you will discover you are not your emotions or your thoughts, but something more.

In the DBT space, there's something known as the emotion mind. What this means is that your emotions dictate the thoughts that you think. As someone with BPD, you feel like you're constantly being tossed about by intense feelings that are seemingly beyond your control. You go along with them, with very detrimental consequences. Each time you look back on your actions, you can't quite figure out how you got to the point where you reacted the way you did. You find your inability to pay attention makes you more likely to change your mind on account of your feelings, and so you do not keep the commitments you've made to yourself and others. So you find yourself killing relationships, which you value, and saying things you do not mean.

For the most part, people tend to ignore how much of a habit thought patterns are. We never really think about our thinking, because we weren't taught how to do that. This is where mindfulness can help again. If your mind is not trained, it can cause you a lot of pain and heartache without you even being aware of it. Like a pendulum, you swing from one extreme to the other. You either get so enmeshed in your mind that you pay way too much attention to certain thoughts, or you worry to the point of obsession and are unable to see past your nose. Either way, you don't pay attention to your thinking habits. It almost seems to you that things tend to unfold on their own, and you have no power over the way you react. I don't need to tell you how being on one extreme or the other can cause you issues, and suffering. Mindfulness will help you grow in curiosity, awareness, and attention. This is how you'll finally own your mind and break the habits of thought you've got.

The Need for Curiosity and Attentiveness

When you don't develop your attention, and when you're not curious about life, you'll be stuck in your usual routines. Routines may help you avoid the pain you feel, but in the end, they also keep you stuck, and this can add to more pain in the long run. It never pays to try to ignore your emotions and thoughts.

You have to pay attention to your thoughts. This means you need to pause every now and then and take an unbiased look at your mind. How fast or slow are you thinking? Are your thoughts a jumbled mess or well put together? Are they loving and kind or angry and resentful? What exactly is it that you're thinking about?

The point of mindfulness is to take charge of your mind and thought processes, and by extension, your emotions. AS you pay attention, the peace and serenity you feel in your life will go up a hundredfold. It might be difficult to believe that mindfulness can help you achieve all this, especially as you've never done it before, but I promise you it works.

The Practice

As you practice, pay attention to how your body and mind feel. This will help you learn all the things you can do to decrease your suffering through your emotions and thoughts. In the DBT space, these actions are known as the "what" and "how" skills — "what" being the actions you take to be mindful, and "how" being the way you go about it.

Try the practices that you will be given in this book at least one time. You'll need a journal, so you can take down notes on your experiences after each practice. You will find that some of the practices feel better for you than others, however, don't stick to them just yet without trying out everything, so that you can tell what works for you and what doesn't. The goal isn't to get you to like the practice, but to encourage you to become more curious, and give your mind a challenge.

I need to point out that some days, you will feel your practice went a lot better than on other days. This does not mean you're failing. It's just the way it is. Today you're breezing through your practice; tomorrow, you're finding the same practice challenging. The beauty of mindfulness is that your experience of it is always dynamic, never static.

One more thing I should mention is that your mind will wander. You must be comfortable with that fact. When you notice your mind has gone off on a tangent, do not beat up on yourself. Noticing is actually progress! So simply bring your mind back to your mindful task, whatever it may be. Each time your mind wanders, and you bring it back, you will get better at maintaining mindfulness. Remember, your mind is like a muscle. This is how it gets stronger.

The Power of Intention

You cannot practice mindfulness without intention. The intention is a beautiful thing, because if you can do something mindlessly, then with intention, you can actually do it mindfully. Intention means you're choosing to pay attention to something, with a specific goal in mind. So you could brush your teeth like always, while your thoughts are on autopilot, wondering about bills and mortgages, or you can spend that time noticing the way you brush, the way your mouth feels, and so on. You notice the desire to think about how to take care of the bills, but then you shift your attention back to the simple act of brushing your teeth. As you brush, your mind will wander off. When it does, you can simply come back to brushing. You can do this with any activity that you do on the regular, whether it's driving, walking, doing the dishes, or laundry. This is how you infuse mindfulness in your daily activities.

There is a misconception that the whole point of mindfulness is to have a mind that never wanders. That's impossible. You will always have thoughts in your head. That's the function of your brain. What mindfulness is, is intentionally choosing to refocus your attention back on the tasks at hand each time your mind wanders. It's not about keeping your mind quiet and empty.

Decide, Commit, Succeed

As you make the decision to practice being mindful, you've got to keep reminding yourself of what you've set out to do and why. It matters that in the beginning, you are clear with yourself about the fact that you're going to be mindful of what the task you've chosen, whether it's doing the dishes or washing your car. Tell yourself you will do this mindfully, and automatically your brain takes a cue that it needs to focus on the task before you. Once you commit this way, you are more likely to succeed.

A Different Practice for Each Day

All you need to do is intend to change at least one of the things you do habitually for every day, just for a week. If you're used to getting out of bed on the left side, try getting out on the right. Do you usually open doors with your dominant hand? Commit to using the other hand. It's all about doing something different for a set period of time and paying full attention to the process.

Observing

Yet another skill the practice of mindfulness will give you is observation. You will begin to simply observe and notice the thoughts you have and the way you feel. In DBT, this is known as the "observe" skill.

In the practice of mindfulness, you're not observing with the goal of passing judgment or labeling things. You're simply paying attention to your experience, without trying to assign it to a box. You experience whatever is happening fully, with all your senses. The challenge here is not labeling anything.

For the most part, we do everything we do without paying much attention to it, and this is why we miss out on very critical bits of information that could make our experience better. As you learn to pay attention, the automatic response you're so used to will become apparent to you. This is particularly useful for those with BPD since a huge part of the problem with BPD is the thoughtless, automatic reactions that cause needless suffering. If you find that there is something or someone to whom you naturally respond with anger, as you become more mindful, you'll notice that it's simply an automatic response you've gotten used to on account of repetition, which has made it a habit. Then you will find that you actually have a choice. You can choose to respond differently, the same way you chose to start lacing your right shoe first before your left in your mindfulness practices.

One more superpower that mindfulness will give you is the ability to notice your emotions in the beginning stages before they fully blossom. Once you're able to tell you're getting sad or angry before you fully give in to the emotion, you will no longer feel as though emotions "just happen" to you. You will realize you're in control. You'll realize that at any point in time, you can redirect your emotions. No longer will you be ambushed by intense emotions.

Simply observing is an amazing way to calm your mind. Now, this can be quite a challenge, especially as you will not need words. We tend to assign words to everything we experience. For practice, simply try being outside by yourself, noticing the sights and sounds, without actually assigning any words to them. In the beginning, this will not be easy. Can you just imagine seeing a red rose, without the need to call it "a red rose" in your mind? It's not easy at first, but over time, you get better at it. As you simply observe with no labeling or judging, the part of your mind responsible for thinking will quiet down, and shut off. This is the part of your mind that gets hyperactive whenever you feel anxious or stressed out. The simple act of watching, observing, and noticing, will calm both your body and mind immensely. It involves moving from a state of action, doing, and thinking, to a simple state of being, unconditioned by anything internal or external.

Chapter 8.   Building   A   Coping   Skills Toolkit.

We all have good days and we all have bad days. Experiencing either can be far more intense if you have BPD. A coping skills set will be worth building to help you quickly find ways to deal with bad (or several) days as they arise. Think of this as your Coping Skills Toolkit. This doesn't have to be a physical toolkit, most of the contents will be conceptual anyway, but you can build a list of "items" to go into this kit and carry it around with you. Sometimes when you are overwhelmed with emotion it can be difficult to remember exactly what your coping skills are, or to think clearly about anything. By keeping your list close to hand you can quickly find a way to deal with your emotions. Below is a list of the types of things you can include.

Grounding skills. Very similar to the above these can simply help you to focus on immediate physical and mental stimuli. Use visual or auditory stimulus to take your mind off the immediate negative emotion. Listen to the sounds around you, not just the obvious, but all the sounds that you can hear. Listen to the way in which they rise and fall – so in a busy street you'll hear the roar of traffic, snippets of conversation, birdsong (perhaps) or the sounds of nearby construction work. As long as it's safe, lose yourself in just the sounds around you for a moment.

Journal keeping. This is a practice that many with BPD find useful for establishing triggers, evaluating emotions and creating lists of pros and cons. Be expressive in your writing, say whatever you want to and everything that you feel. Sometimes simply expressing yourself in this way can get rid of negative thoughts, without risking alienating others! Don't ever worry about details like spelling, grammar or even making sense. Rant on paper as much as you like!

Positive actions. Think of useful activities to displace your negative emotions. Cleaning the house/oven or sitting and doing some knitting! In fact, anything that is repetitive and requires concentration is an excellent way to manage your emotions and to reduce your intense experience of these.

These are only very basic ideas for you Coping Skills Toolkit. They can be useful for many people but you may also need to find your own ways to cope with the ups and downs of BPD. The important thing to do is list them, keep them with you and build as long a list as you can. Find activities that you can do when you are in the safety of your own home (knitting, for example) and ones that you can do when you are out and about or at work (simple mindfulness, for example). Have a good mix of these so that whatever the situation you can find a simple coping skill that will be suitable for the situation.

Once you've got your list, practice; not all of the skills will come naturally to you and you may need to persevere with some until they do. By practicing you are also reinforcing good skills in your mind and they will be there when you need them. Over time you'll find that your natural reaction to emotional situations is to use one of your new skills, rather than to take the former, self-destructive route. This, as mentioned at the start of the book, is the point where your BPD will begin to be less of a daily issue and you will be well on the way to recovery.

BPD and Self-Esteem

In most cases of BPD you'll find that low self-esteem is part of the scenery! In many instances BPD begins in adolescence and is the result of neglect or abuse. This is quite frequently emotional neglect and the result of being taught that your views or emotions are not valid. People experiencing low self-esteem often feel that they have little to offer to others or the world in general. There are a number of ways in which to build or rebuild your self-esteem and in this section we'll look at some basic methods. While these are basic you should consider using all of them regularly. Gradually building a sense of self-worth is a hard process and can take a long time. These exercises and tasks are small enough to complete easily, regularly and without being too challenging or onerous. As you succeed in each (frequently and regularly) you'll find yourself building a sound foundation for feelings of self-worth and also that you are tackle bigger projects or tasks which further build on this.

Positive Self-Talk. How do you describe yourself, to yourself? "I'm such an idiot"? "I'm a waste of space"? "I'm not worth knowing"? We all feel like this sometimes but these feelings don't build your self-esteem. It's common when things go wrong to use this kind of "self-talk", more so for those with BPD. Positive self-talk is about repositioning these feelings. You forgot an important appointment? "I've messed up, these things happen!" might be a better statement to make to yourself. "Oh well, it's not the end of the world" is another good one - and it's true. So far, nobody alive (or dead) has made a mistake that resulted in that outcome and the chances are, if it happens, it won't be your fault. Be a bit kinder to yourself.

Take Control. You don't have to take control of big things to make a difference in life. Tidy a drawer, organize a filing system, redecorate a room. Do something that allows you to plan, then execute, a simple task. Do it step by step so achievements come in one after the other. You can consider bigger projects (like bungee jumps or other personal challenges) as your confidence develops – but small steps are where to start.

Do some charity or voluntary work. This is hugely beneficial, as it's all about giving back to society and feeling useful. This can help you to develop a sense that you have some worth to the world and it also gets you out and about amongst other people. This in itself can be challenging but making new friends and developing broader horizons can be a big boost to your self-esteem.

Finally, go to your therapy sessions. Everything in this book is aimed towards giving you simple, basic ideas to get you through one day at a time with BPD. However, professional therapy sessions will be where you make your biggest progress and they will, if you attend regularly, not only help you to improve yourself esteem, prove that you can take control of the condition but also help to your final recovery.

Last Words

BPD is a common condition but, of all mental or emotional issues, it is one that has the best chances of long term and sustainable recovery. It can take years to recover fully but it's important to set that goal from the start. If you suffer from BDP, or you have recently been diagnosed, it's also important to remember that emotions are not, in themselves, bad. They are important parts of our psychological make-up and essential in our daily lives. Learning to accept them, regulate them and cope with extreme emotions can be hard but it is not an impossible task!

Chapter 9. How To Improve Social Relationships

Not many rules that will assist you with leaving an incredible impression. Pursue the five keys sketched out beneath, and you'll have the option to meet and interface with a wide range of individuals in a social association.

Start light

When first gathering or becoming more acquainted with somebody many individuals will pepper the other individual with an invasion of "talk with style" questions (Where do you live? What do you do? How would you like your activity? And so on.). This sort of discussion isn't just exhausting, however it's fiercely awkward to respond to a torrent of inquiries from someone you don't have the foggiest idea.

So as opposed to leaving the door with these sorts of inquiries, you're in an ideal situation getting this show on the road with some light, sans content talk. You could, for instance, remark on something going on in your condition. Or on the other hand open up with a touch of fun loving prodding (simply make certain to keep a grin all over when you bother her so she can see you're kidding). In case you're not feeling the talk, you can generally begin things off with a commendation – maybe on something the individual is wearing that you find intriguing.

Assemble affinity

In each kind of social association, regardless of whether it's a business arrangement or meeting a young lady at a bar, it's critical to assemble affinity. How would you do this? You can begin by utilizing the "I" viewpoint when you talk about your musings, emotions, and conclusions. For example, instead of saying "b-ball is the best game ever" like it's some goal certainty, state "I love b-ball", and perhaps go into somewhat about what you get from it that makes you love it.

This may appear to be an inconspicuous contrast, yet utilizing this "I" point of view gives individuals a look into your inward world – your contemplations, emotions, and so on. What's more, when you give individuals this more profound look it allows them to consider you to be somebody who encounters indistinguishable feelings from them. This makes a passionate association, which gets individuals to feel a more grounded bond with you.

Be a provider

There's a specific attitude that is going to help you massively in a social association. It tends to be hard to get now and again, however on the off chance that you would individuals will like to associate with you however much as could be expected. That outlook is that of a provider.

In your connections don't hope to "get" anything. Try not to approach a young lady simply hoping to get a number, or connect with a business VIP to make sure he'll show signs of improvement work. In the event that you need to construct a solid association with that young lady so she'll need to date you, or that VIP so he'll need to attach you with a vocation, start by giving worth first. Hope to give the young lady a fun encounter and light up her day. Offer to enable the VIP to beat whatever issue he may be confronting. On the off chance that you maintain your attention on persistently giving with no desire for receiving anything consequently, numerous individuals will feel constrained to give back. That young lady will need to give you her number, and that VIP will need to assist you with getting an incredible line of work. This won't be the situation 100% of the time, yet over the long haul concentrating on what you can give as opposed to what you can get is going to deliver immense profits.

Make yourself powerless

In pretty much every kind of social cooperation individuals are stressed over how they run over. It's amazingly invigorating then when somebody goes along and gives them it's alright to remove that "social veil". That they can quit agonizing over attempting to "look cool" and fit it, and that they can be their bona fide selves and still be acknowledged.

An extraordinary method to open this entryway and show individuals it's alright to unwind, open up, and really act naturally is to lead the pack and make yourself helpless. For instance, in case you're uncertain about something (your weight, how you're dressed, how anxious you feel...) don't attempt to conceal it and expectation no one takes note. Rather, sparkle a major light on it. Bring it up and even ridicule yourself for it (simply don't act naturally belittling). Calling attention to your very own defects and chuckling at them is going to help other people rest easy thinking about their apparent flaws. As a little something extra, this is likewise an extraordinary method to make unbelievably profound affinity.

Keep it positive

There is no sort of social collaboration that is upgraded with a negative frame of mind. The more constructive and peppy you can be in your cooperations, the more individuals will appreciate being with you. Dispositions, all things considered, are infectious. Furthermore, on the off chance that you demand remaining warm and constructive in a social collaboration, it will rub on off the individuals you're with. Furthermore, they will cherish having you around.

Powerful Communication – Improving your Social Skills

Building great associations with others can significantly diminish pressure and tension in your life. Truth be told, improving your social help is connected to better emotional wellness all in all, since having great companions can go about as a "support" for sentiments of uneasiness and low disposition. Be that as it may, for certain individuals their tension can add to their evasion of social circumstances, and keep them from building connections. This is particularly valid in the event that you are socially on edge and frantically need to make companions however are either too dreadful to even consider doing so or are uncertain about how to connect with others.

Lamentably, one of the results of maintaining a strategic distance from social circumstances is that you never have the chance to:

Develop your certainty associating with others

Create solid relational abilities that would expand the opportunity for effective connections

For instance, on the off chance that you fear going to gatherings or asking somebody out on the town, your absence of experience and additionally low certainty will make it much MORE hard to tell how to deal with these circumstances (like what to wear, what to state, and so on.). Regularly, individuals have the essential aptitudes however come up short on the certainty to utilize them. In any case, practice will build your certainty and improve your relational abilities.

Why Are Communication Skills Important?

Relational abilities are the way to creating (and keeping) fellowships and to building a solid social encouraging group of people. They likewise assist you with dealing with your own needs, while being conscious of the necessities of others. Individuals aren't brought into the world with great relational abilities; like some other aptitude, they are found out through experimentation and rehashed practice.

3 regions of correspondence that you might need to rehearse are:

Non-verbal correspondence

Discussion aptitudes

Emphaticness

Note: obviously, there are numerous angles to compelling correspondence and you may need progressively explicit assistance in specific territories (for example figuring out how to manage struggle, introduction aptitudes, giving criticism, and so forth.). For increasingly explicit assistance, if it's not too much trouble see the "Prescribed Readings" list toward the finish of this module.

Non-Verbal Communication

An enormous piece of what we impart to one another is nonverbal. What you state to individuals with your eyes or your non-verbal communication is similarly as amazing as what you state with words. At the point when you feel on edge, you may act in manners that are intended to abstain from speaking with others. For instance, you may stay away from eye to eye connection or talk delicately. At the end of the day, you are doing whatever it takes not to convey, prone to abstain from being judged adversely by others. In any case, your non-verbal communication and manner of speaking communicates amazing messages to others about your:

Passionate state (for example eagerness, dread)

Frame of mind towards the audience (for example accommodation, scorn)

Information on the point

Genuineness (do you have a mystery plan?)

Along these lines, in the event that you are maintaining a strategic distance from eye to eye connection, remaining far away from others, and talking discreetly, you are likely imparting, "Avoid me!" or "Don't converse with me!" Chances are, this isn't the message that you need to send.

Discussion Skills

Probably the greatest test for somebody with social tension is beginning discussions and propping them up. It isn't unexpected to battle a piece when you are attempting to make casual banter, since it isn't in every case simple to consider comments. This is particularly evident when feeling restless. Then again, some on edge individuals go on and on, which can have a negative impact on others.

Self-assuredness

Self-assured correspondence is the genuine articulation of one's own needs, needs and sentiments, while regarding those of the other individual. At the point when you convey decisively, your way is non-compromising and non-critical, and you assume liability for your very own activities.

On the off chance that you are socially on edge, you may have some trouble communicating your contemplations and sentiments transparently. Self-assuredness abilities can be hard to adapt, particularly since being self-assured can mean keeping yourself away from the manner in which you would typically get things done. For instance, you might fear strife, consistently oblige the group, and abstain from offering your suppositions. Accordingly, you may have built up a detached correspondence style. On the other hand, you may expect to control and rule others and have built up a forceful correspondence style.

Be that as it may, an emphatic correspondence style brings numerous advantages. For instance, it can assist you with relating to others all the more truly, with less nervousness and hatred. It likewise gives you more power over your life, and decreases sentiments of powerlessness. Besides, it permits OTHER individuals the privilege to live their lives.

Chapter 10.   How To End Anxiety

No matter what kind of role you play in life, the ability to properly control and express your emotions is sure to play a vital role. You also need to be able to understand, interpret, and respond appropriately to emotions that others around you have as well. Think about how it would be if you weren't able to tell when one of your close friends was feeling sad or when one of your coworkers was mad at you. When you are not only able to express and control your own emotions but also interpret and understand the emotions of others, you are said to have emotional intelligence.

To keep things simple, emotional intelligence refers to your ability to perceive, control, and evaluate emotions whether they are your own emotions or emotions that someone else is feeling. Some people have a high emotional intelligence and are able to control the emotions that they have in many situations while also responding to the emotions of those around them. On the other hand, some people have poor emotional intelligence; these are the individuals who will explode at almost anything and barely take the feelings of others into consideration.

Let's take a look at the difference between someone who has emotional intelligence and someone who doesn't. Our first person is someone who takes life as it comes. They realize that most of the time when things go wrong, it is out of their control rather than seeing it as the world attacking them directly. They rarely get upset, especially over the little things and know the proper times to show their emotions.

In addition, this person responds well to how others are feeling. When a coworker comes and starts yelling at them, they don't respond in kind. They realize that something must really be bothering that person and they step up to try and help or correct the issue at the heart of the problem. When one of their friends is having a bad day, they talk through it and help that friend feel better.

Now, let's look at our second person. This person has a hard time controlling their emotions. When they are upset about something, they will explode at others (whether it is that other person's fault or not), they cry easily, and they may have anxiety. These individuals will often have the idea that the world is against them and little things, the things that don't matter that much, will set them off.

When it comes to responding to others, this is barely a thought. They will ignore the feelings of their friends and only process events based on how they are personally affected by them. When someone else is mad at them they think that they are being unfairly treated. The world is against them and everyone just doesn't understand them.

The first person we met is someone who has a high level of emotional intelligence. This person knows how to recognize and control their emotions and can even hone in on some of the emotions of others around them. The second person has a low level of emotional intelligence. They get upset over everything, probably have no idea why they feel the way they do, and they don't even pay attention to the feelings of others. Of course, there are variations that happen between these two extremes and figuring out your own level of emotional intelligence can be important for helping you to improve.

Some people believe that you are able to improve your own emotional intelligence with some hard work. But there are others who believe that this is an inborn characteristic, something that you are born with which makes it extremely difficult, if not impossible to change. There is probably a grain of truth to both schools of thought. We are all born with a natural level of emotional intelligence which we can then either nurture and improve or let it grow fallow through disuse.

The four parts of emotional intelligence

There are four main factors that are going to determine your emotional intelligence. These include:

• Perceiving emotions: the first thing that you need to do in order to understand emotions is to learn how to perceive them properly. This can include learning how to recognize nonverbal signals like facial expressions and body language.

• Reasoning with emotions: the next thing that you need to do is use your emotions as a way to promote cognitive activity. This can be hard at first, but emotions can help prioritize what we are paying attention to and reacting to, and we can pay attention to this to learn something about ourselves.

• Understanding emotions: there are many meanings that can come with the emotions that we perceive. For example, if you observe that someone is angry, you may have to take a step back and see why they feel the way they do. A boss may be mad at you for your work because they got in trouble with their boss, they fought with their wife, they got a speeding ticket, or for a whole host of other reasons and someone with a high level of emotional intelligence will be able to recognize this.

• Managing emotions: next is the ability to effectively manage your emotions. You need to be able to regulate your emotions, find an appropriate response, and then respond as an important part of your emotional management.

There are several ways that you are able to measure your emotional intelligence. There are some tests that can be done to check on this, but it is also possible to figure out your own emotional intelligence and change it through hard work and perseverance. By learning how to recognize your emotions, what is causing them, and the appropriate response to the situation at hand, you can easily improve your own emotional intelligence in less time than you might think.

So why would you want to spend your time working on emotional intelligence? There are actually quite a few situations in your life where a high level of emotional intelligence can make a big difference. For example, in the workplace. Employees who have a higher level of emotional intelligence are the ones who perform better because they pick out jobs that they are passionate about, do better with other employees, persuade other people to their ideas, and also avoid conflicts. Think about how some of these skills could help you in your own career, whether you are trying to advance or just stay on top. Everyone could use a brush up on these skills to help them do better in the workplace.

Another crucial area where you will really see the benefit of working with emotional intelligence is in your relationships, whether these are with a partner, with your family, or even your co-workers. Each person that you encounter is going to have their own feelings and being able to recognize these and respond in the proper way will make it so much easier for you to get along with them. When conflict does arise, you will be able to keep your emotions in check, preventing a bigger blowout than is necessary no matter what kind of relationship you are trying to work on.

Emotional intelligence is something that everyone is able to improve upon and there are so many benefits to so. However, it is important to realize that it is also a skill that takes some time to master. You will not be able to wake up after practicing for a day or two and have total control over your emotions. In fact, this is probably something that you will have to work on for quite some time before it becomes a habit. But when you understand this from the start and work hard to observe, understand, and manage your emotions you will be able to reach your goals in no time.

Common difficulties in using the EMDR method

Q.: I do not have time to simultaneously present an unpleasant picture and move my eyes.

A.: You do not have to think about the picture while you are making eye movements. You focus on it at the beginning, and then you can completely concentrate on the movements themselves and upon their completion return to the picture again.

Q.: I chose one picture for study, but after the first round of movements, another one appeared in front of my eyes, also unpleasant, but connected with a completely different situation. Should I continue to work on the original picture or take on a new one?

A.: In such cases, it's recommended trusting your internal process. If a new picture has arisen spontaneously, it is worth working with it. Exercise it until it ceases to cause any discomfort. After that, return to the originally selected goal with which you started work.

Q.: I do not remember the situation completely. I have only a vague or fragmentary memory.

A.: Absolute accuracy is not required at all. Take in the work that material is available to you at the moment. Even fragmentary memories can be effectively worked out with the help of EMDR. In some situations, after 2-3 rounds of EMDR, the picture takes on more specific outlines, and additional details that you did not remember before may begin to appear in it. But this is not necessary. When you can't remember the situation completely, pay more attention to the feelings that it causes you.

Q.: After 2 rounds of EMDR, the picture remained unchanged, and the intensity of unpleasant sensations only increased.

A.: This is really possible: the process of working through negative information occurs through a temporary intensification of an unpleasant feeling. This is natural and happens when a person tries to keep an unpleasant feeling at a distance from himself. When working with the EMDR method, (similar to working with EFT) it is important not to resist the unpleasant sensations associated with the images that you are working on.

Q.: The intensity of the sensations is too high. When I try to work out the situation, I have such strong feelings that I just can't continue. I am afraid that in this case I will become even worse.

A.: In such a situation, use the technique of emotional freedom (EFT) in order to relieve the senses and stabilize your condition. Perhaps you still have too few resources to work out precisely this traumatic moment. In this case, temporarily postpone work with this episode. While working out less difficult memories for you, use EFT to learn how to better regulate your current state - all this will allow you to increase your stress resistance resource. After a while, you will be able to return to working out the hardest memories. An alternative is to seek professional help from a specialist who has experience working with severe emotional injuries.

Chapter 11.   What Does It Mean To Rewire Your Brain?

It's crucial to understand the following fact: It's not life circumstances that prevent us from achieving what we want, nor is it the way our brains are made. It is how we have trained our minds to think and react. We are our own biggest enemy!

Cognitive Fusion

Cognitive fusion is the linking of thoughts to experiences. Say you are in an elevator that stalls midway down or up. You're stuck inside for a few minutes and understandably, you start to panic. But the problem is quickly fixed and the elevator continues on its way and you reach your destination safe and sound. It's a scary experience, yes; but the odds of it happening again are very slim indeed. However, the next time you enter an elevator, you remember the experience; your brain remembers how you reacted and once again, you will feel panic. Unless you intervene and train your mind to react differently, this will happen each time you get into an elevator and over time, it will become a phobia. This is called cognitive fusion. The experience becomes "fused" to a particular reaction to your brain. In other words, your mind forms a habit.

Now, you have two choices here. Either you avoid elevators altogether (not an appealing option when you have an important job interview on the 15th floor), or, retrain your mind to react differently. You can use cognitive fusion to work for you instead of against you.

Cognitive fusion occurs when the mind starts to interpret thoughts as facts. In this example, it believes that when you step into an elevator, it will stall. And because you reacted with fear and panic the first time this happened, your brain believes you are in danger. It will warn you of this danger by triggering again those feelings of fear, anxiety and panic. It looks like your brain is actually trying to help you based on the information YOU gave it the first time this happened!

In cognitive fusion, the mind "fuses" the thought to the experience and reacts in the same way each time that experience is repeated. It does this with both positive and negative experiences. For example, let's say you are at the beach and witness an amazing sunset over the ocean. You experience feelings of wonder, joy and tranquility as you watch the beautiful colors spread across the horizon and slowly fade. Your brain perceives the sunset is a positive experience that makes you feel good and will trigger those same feelings each time you see a sunset until they become fused to the experience.

Can you see how we might unknowingly train our minds to harm and hinder rather than help? The other side of the coin is that we can also train our brain to help rather than hinder. Realizing that we can rewire our mind to react the way we want it to is a life-changing concept. Let's continue a bit more with our exploration of the brain.

The Cortex and the Amygdala, Two Anxiety pathways

Why do we experience anxiety and worry?

The human brain has the unique ability to imagine the future. No other living creature can do this (which is, perhaps, a blessing in disguise!). However, many of us tend to envision adverse rather than positive outcomes, especially when we are under stress. As a result, we become anxious or worried. Again, we train our brain to perceive the future as something bas or harmful and this trigger negative thoughts and emotions.

Anxiety is created in the brain through two "anxiety pathways", the cerebral cortex and the Amygdala. They are located in different areas of the brain but their function is similar.

The Amygdala

This is an almond-shaped cluster of neurons found deep inside the temporal lobe. It is responsible for processing thoughts and emotions that have to do with survival, such as fear, anger, pleasure and anxiety. It also determines where memories are stored on the brain based on the strength and type of emotions involved on the experience that creates the memory.

The amygdala cannot prove itself unlike between actual events and thoughts, and responds to both in the same way. For example, if you are in real danger it will trigger a "fear and flight" response to help you avoid or confront the danger. Likewise, if you 'think' a certain situation is dangerous when there is no real danger, the amygdala will trigger the very same fear and flight response.

The Cerebral Cortex

The cerebral cortex is a very thin layer ranging between 1.5 mm. to 5 mm. that covers the cerebrum. It is commonly referred to as "gray matter" because the nerves are not insulated making it appear gray, unlike the other parts of the brain which appear white. It is responsible for several functions, including determining personality and intelligence, planning an organization, language processing and sensory functions and motor functions. The cortex also helps us to experience and interact with our world.

An example of cortex-based anxiety is when in certain situations, our mind jumps ahead and envisions a negative outcome. Let's say you receive a phone call from someone who hasn't contacted you in a long time. You immediately imagine that the caller has bad news, perhaps a death in the family, and you start to feel worried and anxious. Instead, the person is calling to invite you to a wedding. This is how the cortex works to trigger anxiety.

Controlling the Cortex and the Amygdala

You can control the negative emotions triggered by the cortex and amygdala simply by controlling your thoughts. Always remember that your mind is not the culprit; it is simply responding to the thoughts you feed it. Psychologists who specialize in this field advise us to stand up to our thoughts, and to challenge them. Is that elevator really going to stall every time you step into it? Is it really likely to happen again? Probably not. Therefore, the fear and panic are irrational. Pessimists especially need to do this and realize that their thoughts do not and cannot control the future. Exchanging negative thoughts for positive ones will not control the future either, but having an optimistic outlook makes life so much better!

Cognitive Restructuring

The first step in the process of rewiring your mind is to step back and observe a certain thought. Do not try to push it away but don't yield to it or believe it either. Simply acknowledge the thought. Next, question the thought and finally, challenge it. What evidence do you have that this is going to happen? How likely is it to happen? Are you absolutely sure that this will be the outcome? Is it realistic to suppose that this will be the outcome?

Cognitive restructuring is the process of learning to be suspicious of negative thoughts and to generate opposing thoughts.

Start with your most recurring anxiety and fear-inducing thoughts. Observe, acknowledge, and challenge them. Then, replace them with more realistic thoughts. Doing this repeatedly will literally start the process of transformation - the wiring of your mind will begin to change!

Let's illustrate this with an example. Whenever you receive a utility bill, you start to feel anxious and worried. You're on a tight budget and are afraid it will be too high. What if you can't pay it? What if you can't pay the next one? The bills will keep piling up until your electricity is cut off. You work yourself up into a frenzy of worry, all before opening the bill!

Instead, begin the process of positive restructuring by doing the following: step back from your first thought, that the bill will be too high. Observe and acknowledge the thought... it makes you feel worried and anxious. Now, challenge the thought. Is it reasonable to get so worked up about a utility bill? How do I know for sure it's going to be much higher than what I normally pay? Haven't I always managed to pay my bills before? If worse comes to worst, I can borrow the money, or take it out of my savings, can't I? What's the big deal? When you repeat this process over and over again, there will come a time when that utility bill will arrive and your mind will think, "Oh, it's the utility bill. Okay..." You're not exactly leaping with joy but you're not anxious or worried, either. You can do this with every recurring negative thought that you have.

What Is Self-Awareness?

First of all, you should know what self-awareness actually is. It's being in tune with our inner world and being able to understand our emotions and thoughts as they come.

However, self-awareness is about much more than simply knowing what you're thinking and feeling. It's also about being able to process and deal with that knowledge in a constructive way. It's about using your knowledge to control and alter your thoughts and emotions so they fit with the kind of person you want to become, the situation you're in, and the goals you've set for yourself.

Self-awareness includes knowing:

Your own strengths and weaknesses,

Your motivations,

What makes you happy,

What you want to change about yourself or your life,

How other people see you,

Your beliefs and values.

Your thoughts and feelings.

Self-awareness is the foundational skill for any kind of personal growth or development. In order to be able to change anything about your inner world, you first have to be aware of what's going on in it. Remaining unaware of your thoughts, feelings, and beliefs will cause you to remain stagnant, never really growing or developing in any meaningful way.

Self-Awareness and Self-Esteem

At first glance, it might seem like becoming more aware of your inner world will only lower your self-esteem. After all, being keenly aware of the thoughts and feelings that arise could serve to only reinforce the negative beliefs and feelings you have about yourself. Though it might cause some painful feelings, in the beginning, developing your self-awareness doesn't stop at wallowing in those painful feelings.

Developing self-awareness pushes through them to help you form an objective and accurate view of yourself.

There's a huge difference between self-awareness and self-consciousness. Self-consciousness is being consumed by your own thoughts and feelings, constantly analyzing them critically and judging yourself for them. Women tend to struggle with self-consciousness immensely because society has told us that we need to look and behave a certain way. When a woman doesn't fall in line with that model, it's easy for her to become extremely self-critical and self-conscious, always thinking about what other people think of her.

If you're afraid of this idea of self-awareness because you think it will lead you to judge yourself too much, you can relax a little. Self-awareness is about developing an objective view of yourself. It's about accepting both your strengths and your weaknesses so that you can use your strengths effectively and grow in your areas of weakness. But it is not about being critical of yourself.

For example, someone who is self-conscious might think to themselves: "I'm such a boring, stupid person! I couldn't even come up with one good idea in that meeting." On the other hand, someone who is self-aware might think instead: "I didn't really have anything to add during this meeting, and that's ok. I wonder if I should come with a few prepared ideas next time so I don't have to think of something on the spot?"

See the difference? The self-conscious person becomes upset with themselves, blaming themselves for being stupid and boring. The self-aware person acknowledges that they weren't able to come up with ideas on the spot and forgives themselves for that, then tries to find a practical solution to perform better in the next meeting.

Becoming self-aware won't lower your self-esteem. In fact, you'll be better equipped to raise your self-esteem because you'll have an objective and accurate view of yourself that you can fall back on when you start to feel like you don't measure up. But how do you develop your sense of self-awareness?

5 Ways to Develop Self-Awareness
Give yourself some space

It's very difficult to get in the habit of focusing on your own thoughts and feelings when you're surrounded by a crowd of people. The noise and the social pressures get in the way of being able to simply sit and listen to yourself. So, take some time every day to just sit quietly with yourself. It doesn't have to be a long amount of time—just five minutes every day is a great place to start. Avoid any kind of distraction and spend just a few minutes with your own thoughts before you get up in the morning or go to bed at night.

Practice mindfulness

While you sit with your own thoughts for a few minutes, you could use that time to practice focused, purposeful mindfulness. Instead of allowing your mind to wander and just kind of being there, practicing mindfulness will help you pay attention to the thoughts that arise. You can do this through meditation if you'd like. There are many resources available for getting started with meditation, including apps for smartphones like Headspace or Calm.

Journal every day for self-reflection

Journaling is a great way to learn to pay attention to your thoughts. You can simply sit with a pen and paper and write out the thoughts and feelings you experienced throughout the day. Your journal is not for anyone else's eyes, so you can be as disjointed and all-over-the-place as you need to be. You should also spend a little bit of time purposefully reflecting on your successes and failures for the day and how you can improve for the next day. Keeping a record of your self-reflection is a great way to practice being non-judgmental of yourself and discovering solutions to the mistakes you make throughout the day.

Listen to others to learn their perspectives

Part of being self-aware is understanding how other people perceive you. So take some time to truly listen to some trusted people about what they perceive to be your strengths and weaknesses. Of course, you have to be careful about who you listen to. Some people might try to sugarcoat something you need to work on and others might be overly critical or even mean. It's risky to be vulnerable like this, but if you choose to listen to people who will be objective, honest, and kind, it will be well worth it.

Take a few personality tests

An easy way to gain some really good insight about yourself is to take a couple of trusted and established personality tests. Some of these include the Myers-Briggs Type Indicator and the Enneagram Type Indicator. The official tests will cost a little bit of money, but there are free versions available that are very good.

Reflect

In your own words, describe the difference between self-awareness and self-consciousness.

How self-aware do you think you are?

What is one thing you could start doing today to increase your self-awareness?

Chapter 12. How To Overcome Panic Thoughts

We have looked at various factors that contribute to anxiety and panic attacks. We have had a look at anger and negativity among other factors that contribute to anxiety and panic attacks. In this chapter, we will be focusing on the best ways to deal with anxiety and panic attacks. If you have been suffering from anxiety and panic attacks, you should be ready to move from one phase of your life to another.

With that said, it is important to note that healing from anxiety depends on personal efforts. All the advice and guides provided in this book can only open your eyes. The largest part of the work has to be done by you as an individual. You must stay dedicated to the cause if you wish to enjoy a life that is free from panic attacks and anxiety.

Self-Discovery And Awareness

Self-discovery and awareness refer to the process of determining whether you suffer from a condition or not. In anxiety and panic attacks, sometimes it is difficult for patients to know whether they suffer from such conditions. If you do not know that you are a victim of anxiety, you may never take any action towards it. However, getting to understand that you are a victim gives you the desire to deal with the situation first hand.

Step 1: Start Monitoring your feelings

Monitoring your feelings is a good way to awaken your awareness to the situations around you. Self-awareness will help you determine how you feel about certain people or circumstances. If you are able to categorize your feelings and determine every aspect of your environment that triggers anxiety, you will be on your way to preventing occurrences of panic attacks. It is important to have a clear understanding of your feelings and emotions. This is the first step to self-discovery. In this first step, you only need to start paying attention to your feelings. For instance, you can choose to take a week of self-assessment. When you go to your workplace, monitor your actions. Before you take any action, think about its consequences and try to understand the role played by your emotions in every action you take. Doing this for a whole week will awaken your senses and you will start being aware of your feelings and your environment.

Step 2: Note down your feelings and actions

The next step is to record your feelings and actions. This step is particularly important for individuals who find it difficult to monitor their feelings. If you have tried monitoring your feelings but you keep losing track, writing them down would be a good idea. On a typical working day, set your phone reminder to ring after every 2 hours. In this period, note down all the important decisions you have made and how they are influenced by your feelings. Note down your mood and feelings and also note down the consequences of your actions. At the end of the day, review your feelings in relation to your actions. Mark all the negative outcomes and the positive ones. Do this exercise repeatedly for about 2 weeks and you will realize that negative moods lead to negative decisions. When you are angry or sad, you are likely to make poor decisions. Learning your decision-making flaws should help you stay away from making such poor decisions in the future. You will start understanding your moods and feelings and consequently, start making the right decisions that are not influenced by momentary feelings.

Step 3: Relate your feelings, actions, and consequences

After noting down all the feelings and consequences, relate them to each other. You may even compare the good versus the bad decisions you made when you were in a poor state of mind. This should help you learn to make decisions without getting your emotions involved. When you involve emotions in your decision-making process, a lot of things are likely to go wrong. You have to stick to your sober mind when making important life decisions that may affect your career or family life.

Acceptance and Self Love

The other way of dealing with panic attacks is acceptance and self-love. Most people drown into anxiety because they feel that they are not loved or that they are being targeted by people who hate them. This is all an illusion brought about by a lack of self-love. If you wish to receive the love you crave from the world, you should love yourself first. Self-love gives you the courage to face those who hate you or those who criticize your choices.

Acceptance and self-love are important aspects that will help you tune your mind to the reality of life. If you have been having negative thoughts, you have to get rid of them in order to clear your mind of anxiety. If you have been harboring negative emotions such as anger and hate, you must clean your mind of such in order to enjoy your life. All these aspects of mind refining depend on acceptance and self-love.

Acceptance means that you choose to accept your weaknesses. There are many people who live in denial of their weaknesses. We have noted that some of the causes of negativity include loss, rejection, and betrayal. Such factors can make you get into a state of emotional confusion. The only way to overcome the negativity associated with painful emotional circumstances is acceptance. If something terrible has happened, you must accept that it has already happened. If you lost someone or something, you must accept that the loss has already happened. Trying to fight with facts will not help you in any way. Staying in a state of denial can be devastating on your mind. You need to look at all the facts objectively and determine if there is a way back. If you can recover your losses, you are allowed to try. However, if you realize that the happenings in your life are already out of control, do not try forcing things to work in a certain way. Trying to force life to workout according to your preferences will only give you more pressure. You must learn to accept that in life, there will be times when you win and times when you lose. You must accept that there will be times when you make a profit and times when you make losses. Trying to show yourself to the world as a perfect being will hurt you more than it will hurt anyone else. Do not try standing out or showing the world that you are too strong. Accept the difficult situations and move on.

The act of moving on after acceptance is filled with self-love. If you cannot love yourself, you cannot move on. It is often difficult for people to move on with life after abuse or failure. Most people may try to hang around trying to make things work. For instance, if you are rejected by a relationship partner, do not try staying around thinking that things will work out. If someone has blatantly rejected your love, do not beg them to receive it. Show your love to yourself.

Lack of acceptance and self-love often leads to:

Low self-esteem: If you pay too much attention to emotional abuse, loss, failure, rejection, and betrayal, you will realize that you lose trust in yourself. All these painful emotional instances may make you feel as if you are a failure in life and that you do not deserve to live a good life. However, if you choose to accept your situation and determine in your mind to love yourself despite the situation, you will come out of every situation stronger than you got into it.

Comparison: If you feel that you are not good enough, it is because you have been comparing yourself to others. Comparison is a product of denial. If you start looking at yourself thinking that you should be at the same level as the other person, you may eventually develop hatred for yourself. This will lead to low self-esteem and as a result, you may start blaming yourself and the people around you for your failures.

Low self-esteem and shifting blame will definitely lead to a lack of trust. You will start thinking that the people around you are ridiculing your actions. You start perceiving friends as enemies; as a result, you may end up experiencing depression, anxiety, panic attacks among other mental inconsistencies.

Meditation

The other way of dealing with anxiety and panic attacks is through meditation. There are many techniques for meditation that can be used to improve your feelings, your thoughts and your social life as a whole. For the purposes of this book, we will only be focussing on two types of meditation: Mindfulness and peace love meditation.

Meditation is a technique where you choose to focus your mind on a specific area of life. When a person performs meditation, the mind is engaged through a visualization process. Meditation helps the practitioner confine in a safe place. It transports your life from the realities that cause you pain and takes you to a place where you feel at peace.

Meditation is an ancient technique that has been around for several decades. Long before our current era, people used meditation for curative purposes. You can use meditation to cure emotional and even physical pain. When a person meditates, the mind is transformed and helped to release important chemicals that are vital for the relaxation and functioning of body organs. Meditation also enhances the flow of blood in the body, allowing your body to undergo full metabolism.

Mindfulness: Mindfulness is a meditation technique where the practitioner focuses on themselves. For instance, if you are the one performing meditation, you have to focus on yourself. Mindful meditation is a wide subject. When focusing on yourself, you may choose to focus on your thoughts, your physical body parts, your painful areas, your emotions or any other part of your body. This means that you need to take a lot of time learning mindfulness meditation. For beginners, you are encouraged to focus on your breath or close your eyes and focus on your blood flow.

Simple mindfulness meditation

Step 1: Find the perfect spot

Mindfulness meditation, just like all the other types of meditation should be done in a calm and quiet place. To get started, find a location that is calm and quiet. The meditation process should take between 10 minutes and 1 hour. Depending on the length of your session, ensure that your tranquil location will remain quiet for a long time. You do not want intruders coming in when you are at the center of your meditation.

Step 2: Collect all the essential

You will need some essentials during your meditation. For mindfulness meditation, the only important essential is a meditation mat or a chair. If you choose to use a chair, make sure it has an upright back.

Step3: Position yourself

When you are ready to start your meditation, position yourself accordingly. Mindfulness is performed when the practitioner is sitting in an upright position. You may sit on your mat with legs crossed in from of you and your arms on your laps or, you may sit in your chair uprightly. Ensure that you feel comfortable and that you can breathe freely.

Step 4: Close your eyes and focus on your breath

With your eyes closed, now focus your thoughts on your breathing. Feel the air come in and go out without trying to control it. Let your mind just focus on your breath until your full concentration is on your breath. It should take you about 5 minutes to get your mind focused. If you realize that your mind keeps on wandering off, try focusing your mind again. For beginners, it might take longer than 5 minutes to get your mind focused.

Step 5: Advance to specific body parts

After you have mastered the art of meditation by focusing on your breath, you should be ready to move your mindfulness to the next level. Do not try moving to this level before you are sure that you can meditate by focusing on your breath. During the first few days, you should only focus on your breath. As you advance, start focusing on other parts of the body. In advanced levels, you may choose to focus on your body shape. In your mind, visualize your body shape, your weight and the general alignment of your body. This allows you to know what you like about your body and whatever you do not like. You may also choose to focus on your thoughts. Mindfulness meditation allows you to see your deepest desires. You can see your thoughts, what you think about life and what you think about love. All these aspects will help you know who you are and why you make the decision you do in daily life,

Why mindfulness meditation is important for anxiety and panic attacks patients.

I) Mindfulness is practiced in a non-judgmental space: The first rule for anyone who wishes to practice mindfulness is that you must be non-judgmental. As we have seen, mindfulness will unravel the dirtiest secrets about your desires. When you practice mindfulness, you will note a lot of bad things about yourself that you may not want to show to the world. The only way to practice mindfulness and remain happy is by living a non-judgmental life. People who suffer from anxiety and panic attacks are generally judgmental. They are hard on themselves and others. Anxiety patients judge others based on their appearances, race or gender. They are quick to crucify people and label them as either dangerous or harmful. However, when you practice mindfulness, you get to learn the act of being non-judgmental.

II) Mindfulness practitioners are self-aware: The other reason why people get into anxiety and panic attacks is that they do not know what they feel or desire. If you do not know your feelings or desires, you may easily be provoked by occurrences around you. However, mindfulness allows you to know yourself in detail. You get to know your likes and desires in detail. When you practice mindfulness nothing will surprise you. You will know the people to avoid and how to handle your triggers.

III) Mindfulness encourages self-acceptance: When you practice mindfulness, you learn to accept your strengths and weaknesses. This is a very important aspect for anxiety and panic attacks patients. Most people suffering from panic attacks do not know how to love themselves. They suffer from low self-esteem and look at themselves as weak creatures. If you practice mindfulness meditation, you start learning about your strengths and the capacity to fight all your enemies.

IV) Peace and Love Meditation: Peace and love meditation is the other technique that you can use to deal with anxiety and panic attacks. Peace and love meditation is very different from mindfulness. In mindfulness, every aspect of your thoughts rotates about your feelings and your being. In peace and love meditation, you are the source of peace and love to the world. You need to look at yourself as the central piece in the world where love extends from to the rest of the world. In this type of meditation, you focus on making the rest of the world happy. When you are the center of peace and love, you look at yourself as the one person who has been given the responsibility to make people happy.

In peace and love meditation, you extend love and peace even to your enemies. Teleport yourself to a beautiful world where everybody is made to smile because of your love.

How to practice peace and love meditation.

Step 1: Find your location and prepare the area

When you want to practice peace and love meditation, you have to prepare the room in the same way we did with mindfulness meditation. Just ensure that you pick a quiet place and have your essentials. You may use a chair or a mat as it is the case with mindfulness meditation.

Step 2: Position yourself and focus your thoughts

You will also have to position yourself on the mat or on the chair, in the same manner, you did with the mindful technique. Make sure you are positioned in an upright manner on your mat or your chair. Now close your eyes and focus on your breath. This will help you focus on your thoughts. For about 5 minutes, just breathe normally with your mind focussed on your breath. After 5 minutes, change your focus from your breath to the darkness. With your eyes closed, there should be a cloud of darkness before you. Just close your eyes and focus on the darkness. Do not think about anything else except for the darkness for about 5 minutes.

Step 3: Focus on your enemies and give them love

In this step, you have to choose one person you deem your enemy. Focus on that person and choose to give them love. Visualize yourself as being the source of happiness for your enemy. In your mind, speak to your enemy in the most loving way possible. Reason with your enemy and even give them gifts. You need to look at yourself as a center if love. Be the person who pours out love to the world, teaching them how to love. Just visit your enemy with a smile and show them that life is beautiful.

Chapter 13.   Conversational Skills

Tips to have a conversation
Make small talk.

Sociologists have a rule that indicates that the best way to create a fluid conversation is to keep one important rule in mind: 30% talking and 70% listening. This is a general rule, and obviously, it will change from situation to situation, so keep that in mind. But in general terms, this will make you an interesting person to talk to, because you will pay attention and ask correct and specific questions. This, in due time, will make you a desirable person to talk to.

At the end of a conversation, don't forget to introduce yourself

This is only applicable if it is a first-time conversation, but it is a great way to ensure that the other person knows and remembers your name. Try to say something like "By the way, I'm…" More often than not, the other person will do the same. Always remember names, because that is a great way to make impressions on people. You will be more inclined to talk to someone who remembered your name or anything else that you told them. Also, if you remember their name, you will not only look smart and intelligent, but they will see that you were paying attention.

Ask them out for coffee

We talked about this tip before, but it is important to expand on this. A social gathering gives you a better opportunity to truly know another person, in a way that perhaps might not be possible in another context. Invite them to get some coffee or to go to the theater. To organize and plan with them, you can give them your phone number or email address. This gives them the possibility to contact you at any time. Don't worry if they don't give you their information in return, because that's fine. There will be time for that in the future, once you get to know each other. One handy way to extend your invitation is to say something along the lines of "I gotta go, but what about we go out some time, maybe to get coffee or for lunch? Here's my phone number if you ever want to call me." Perhaps they don't have enough time to make new friends. I mentioned this before - don't take it personally. Offer your contact information to people who have the potential to be a good friend, and in time, somebody will get back to you.

Dull Conversations

Congratulations, the guy you talked to called to see if that invitation for coffee was still on. You have a new friend! So you both decide on a date, place, and activity. The appointment comes, you sit down to talk and get to know each other, and then you notice that the conversation dies as soon as one of you stops talking. No matter how hard you both try, ultimately, the conversation dies. Even if you go back to your main passion (the one you talked about the first time), the dullness and repetitiveness bore you both. After a while, one of you decides to call it a night and go home. You go home confused. What happened?

Everything seemed to be going great the first time, what happened the second time?

- Abortion and health-related topics

- Religion (this is quite an important one, particularly because many people see religion as a way of life, so, unless you both share the same religion, try to avoid this one at all cost)

- Politics

- In some cases: Sports

While the rest might be quite obvious, you might be thinking that sports shouldn't be on that list, but the truth is that many people take sports way too seriously and will defend their colours or team with a passion. Unless you are knowledgeable on the subject, it's best to stay away from this topic.

Other subjects might be off the table depending on the case (for example, if you see that your interlocutor has a disability, don't bring that up unless the subject comes up naturally), but in general terms, the list should help you stay clear of any problems. With that being said, if your values are rooted in those subjects (you might have a firm opinion on abortion or current politics), always be aware that while people might have an opinion on it, it does not mean that they necessarily want to share it.

We talked about finding out what the other person loves. One quick way to break the social rule or norm that might rule over the conversation (like small talk) is to stop using social scripts or if possible, avoid asking questions that society makes us feel like we need to ask. To do this, go out of your way to learn about that person's life:

- "What has been the best part of your year?"

- "What do you as a hobby?"

- "Leaving work aside, what is your main objective during the day?"

According to several researchers on the topic, what guides our relationships and our interaction with the rest of the world is to feel important, to feel cherished, and to find other interesting people. This is normal, and this does not mean that we are all selfish (although if you need this a bit too much, you may end up having an egocentric personality, so be careful). The psychology behind this is quite straightforward: if you can make someone feel unique and special by listening and paying attention to their opinions, feelings or ideas, you will in turn become attractive to them.

When you talk to someone and want to show them your appreciation, you can try to ask them questions to find out what they believe to be significant. When they give you an answer, you can push their ideas a little further. This is tricky: Let's say that you ask them about what they love the most in the world. Their answer is "Carpentry". In this particular case, you could ask them why and how that thing or action (Carpentry) is important for them. But this does not mean that you can push them around. Don't go hard on them. Remember, you are trying to be interesting, so avoid being aggressive.

If you are talking to someone at a party, try to commit to them entirely. Don't stay on your phone or talk to anyone other than the person you are talking to at that moment. If you dedicate your entire attention to that specific person, they will feel important and worthy of attention and do their best to earn it. Smile if it is a good story, laugh if it is funny, or show sadness if it is a sad story. Don't take a trip to the bathroom so you can check emails or upload a picture to the internet. People will eventually realize this and may stop talking to you. After all, their time is important, so why would they bother with someone who doesn't value it?

Your posture is also a window into your interest in the other person. People unconsciously pick up body signs that show us that people pay attention to them, or that they are ignoring them. Other than avoiding to check your phone, the following are several tips that you might not know about:

The direction of your toes. Yes, it sounds quite silly, but as I said, this is one of those signs that we pick up without even knowing. If you keep your toes pointed to the person speaking, their brains will pick up your feet direction and use that sign to gauge interest. If you are listening to someone talk about their experiences as a father, you can make them feel valued and worthy of your attention by keeping your torso and toes pointed at them while they speak. It's a non-verbal way to express interest and say "go on, I'm listening".

The triple nod is a way of expressing interest. It might sound weird at first, but studies have proved that people tend to speak two to four times longer if you give them a triple nod. This works as a subconscious cue to keep going and expand their story. When someone finishes talking, and you feel that there might be more in it, look at them in their eyes and nod three times. More times than not, they will continue their story, and if they don't, you can always ask another question related to what they have been talking about.

If you see that the conversation is dying, ask open-ended questions. This will help to keep the conversation alive. For example, let's say that your interlocutor is talking about old Roman History, and you see that the discussion is reaching a phase where both of you don't know what to say. In that case, ask something that might take a while to fully answer. In the example that we were talking about, ask about the differences between Romans and Greeks, and how each civilization adapted to the other. Keep in mind that I'm just giving random examples based on conversations that I had in the past, and you can always ask whatever you want. This will help to avoid "yes" and "no" answers, allow your interlocutor to express himself, and share more information that you can use to continue the conversation.

Perhaps this is the perfect time to mention it, but conversations shouldn't be like a police interrogation. While a bit of questioning is fine, it can't be at the expense of your interlocutor's peace. I suggested furthering the conversation a bit more, but never push it to the point that you make the other person feel uncomfortable. If they don't want to answer a question, or they wish to go somewhere else to talk or do something else, let them be. They don't owe you an answer, and if they don't want to speak, they are under no obligation to do so. During my times reading and watching people interact, I've seen several awkward people forcing their views and their opinions over the rest because they wrongly believed that the primary goal of any conversation is to win the argument. This is an absolute mistake and one you should avoid at all costs.

Other things that you can use to start and keep a conversation alive is to talk about something special that they are wearing or something particular about the environment you are both in. In the story that I told you before, my friend's wife asked her about the t-shirt. This is a perfect way to start a conversation because if they are wearing a unique piece of clothing, they will be more inclined to talk about it. Or if they have another unique piece of clothing, like special earrings, for example, it can spark a conversation about where they got them and if they got them during a trip overseas. However, if they don't have anything in particular, you can always comment on your environment, and use it as a cue to talk about anything that comes to your mind. Say that at the party that you are both in, there are distinctive candles lighting up the place. In that case, you can comment that they remind you of the candles that your grandmother used to use (or whatever it tells you; of course, you do not have to follow precisely what I write here!). This, in turn, will create a snowball effect in the conversation and keep the ball rolling.

Keep practicing these steps, and with enough practice, you will see that in every conversation that you have, you will end up going far more in-depth than you expected.

But let's go down the negative road: No matter what you try, the conversation dies. You did everything you could, and you have to understand that you are under no obligation to like every single person you meet in your life. You may create a lasting relationship with some of them, and the rest will come and go from your life. That is okay, and the best solution in these cases is to retreat and move over to another person who you might feel more connected to or have more things in common with.

Keep the Conversation Going Past the Pleasantries

One of the most terrifying things about being in a conversation, especially with strangers, is the awkward silence many of us experience after engaging in a fair amount of small talk.

The awkward silence is something that causes many not to take the plunge into conversation. Now that you have overcome the fear of talking to strangers, introduced yourself in the nicest way possible, and through conversation starters engaged in a fair amount of small talk, the next challenge is the challenge of never running out of things to say. How do we continue the conversation while keeping it interesting and flowing?

To overcome this problem, the first thing you need to understand is why the awkward silence happens, especially when you are conversing with strangers. The awkward silence is internal because when you think you have run out of things to say that is exactly what is happening. You have activated a filter that sifts through what you think is good enough to say to a stranger thus limiting your choices.

This filter is almost nonexistent when you are conversing with people you know well. You can converse for hours about different unrelated topics without stressing over what to say next. Your "good enough for conversation" threshold is very low when speaking to a friend or acquaintance. If you feel like bringing up an interesting topic that pops into your mind, you just do.

Therein lies the answer to keeping a conversation going past the pleasantries. You must lose your inhibitions and not filter things out of your conversation. As long as a topic or thought is good enough to vocalize, do so. You need to learn how to adapt to conversations on the go, which you can do by removing this filter.

In addition to keeping the conversation going past the small talk and pleasantries, you need to be emotionally vulnerable. This does not mean you need to reveal your deepest darkest secret. All it means is that you have to lead first by opening up first. Be the first one to move the conversation past the pleasantries by sharing something personal. Here is why this is important.

You will pick up a few things about the other person when you are attentive. Even so, you cannot outright ask a stranger to tell you his or her darkest secrets. After all, you would not expect someone you just met to ask the same of you. You are likely to be more trusted when you are vulnerable and share

something about yourself to the other person first. When people feel trusted, they reciprocate in kind. Because you have opened yourself up to them, they will open themselves up to you, which will take the conversation deeper.

Learn How to Turn Strangers Into Friends

The greatest of things come to those who are willing to risk rejection and failure. The fear of rejection is the very thing that has been keeping you from creating lasting friendships and relationships with strangers. Now that you have implemented steps 1 through 5, you have overcome this fear. Congratulations! You are now ready for the challenge of turning one off chance conversation with a stranger into a lasting friendship. Here is how to do that:

Build on the Commonalities

At this point, we shall assume that the stranger you want to turn into a friend is someone you have engaged in small talk, and after deepening the conversation, matching and mirroring, have decided that this person is someone worth making a friend.

To keep this conversation going and the friendship flourishing, you can build on commonalities. For instance, if both you and the stranger/acquaintance like hiking, and you and several other friends have planned a hike in the coming weeks or month, you can casually invite this person and then continue deepening the conversation on this point of mutual interest. Because the person likes hiking, he or she is more likely to say yes, and this will offer you a chance to meet the person for a second time. This future interaction will cement the acquaintance and turn it into a budding friendship.

Don't Forget the Contact Information

After having a great first conversation with someone you just met, before you go your separate ways, read the situation. If you feel that the person had a great time conversing with you (especially if, in the earlier example, the person agrees to come for the planned hike), take the initiative and ask for contact information.

Having contact information of your "new friend" is going to make communication easier for when you plan to meet up again. When it comes to asking for contact information, just be direct. Say something like, "I had so much fun chatting with you. Before you go, let's exchange numbers so we can get together and chat more about that hike."

Be Friendly

In more than one occasion, we have indicated that acquaintances feel more attracted to us, and thus more open to friendships, if we are open and vulnerable at a personal level. This is what we mean by being friendly. Once you navigate through steps 1-5 of connecting with a stranger, that person is no longer a stranger, he or she is an acquaintance, which is a step away from friendship. Treat such a person as you would treat a friend, which means you should embark on creating a level of honest communication and familiarity while discussing and acting on mutual interests.

Conclusion

Dealing with the facts about borderline personality disorder is not something that anyone wants to deal with. It can be hard on everyone who is involved. The person who is going through this disorder is acting out and behaving in a way that they think they should because this is the only think that they know how to do. On the other hand, the behavior is not going to make any sense to the family and friends who are close to this person because they are the ones who are getting hurt in the process. Feelings can be wounded on either side, but after looking through this guidebook, it is easier to see why the person with this disorder is acting out in the way that they have been for so many years.

This is a complicated disorder and not one that should be taken lightly. The person who has been going through this disorder is going to need all of the help and support that they can get in order to get to a full recovery. It is not an easy process since many of the chemicals and thoughts that are in their own brain are the ones who are influencing the behavior that is there. But treatment is the only way to get them the help that they need to feel better and get back to their normal life with their friends and family.

The friends and family can work together with the person with the borderline personality disorder by offering to be supportive and be there when they are going through therapy. They can also work to get some of their own therapy to ensure that they are doing just fine in the process as well. This is not easy for either, but placing the blame on your loved one is just going to make the whole thing a lot worse to deal with. Being together is the best way for everyone to get through it.

Understanding what is going on with this disorder is often the first step. Most of the families who find out that a loved one has this personality disorder will often become more upset or mad at the person than they were before the diagnosis. This is often due to the fact that they do not understand the disorder and they assume that the person is lying to them, hiding something, or that nothing is actually wrong with them. Not only is the family guilty of this, but the person with the disorder may be feeling the same way which is why they may be so against getting the help they need.

This guidebook is meant to give much of the information that those with the disorder as well as their family members and friends are going to need to make it through this hard time. The person is often trying to get through something troubling that occurred in their childhood and this is not as easy as some may think. It takes a long time, perhaps years or more, to get it figured out, but with the right understanding and support, they are going to make it through just fine. In fact, the majority of those who get the treatment they need and stick with it are able to return to a normal life with their family and friends and they will not have a relapse ever after they are done.

Use this guidebook to get started on your understanding of this disorder. There is a lot to it and sometimes it is easy to get borderline personality disorder mixed up with one of the other disorders that are out there. This guidebook worked to try and get some of the misconceptions straightened out so that it is easier to understand what is going on and how the sufferer can be helped the most. If you or someone you know is going through this disorder, it is best to get them the help that they need right away. Using this guidebook is one of the best ways possible to help them out and get them back to the life that they deserve.

CPSIA information can be obtained
at www.ICGtesting.com
Printed in the USA
LVHW080543021120
670424LV00007B/214